Handing on
the Faith

A Resource for Evangelization

Michael T. Ryan

Solidarity Books

Nihil obstat: Rev. David Boutette
Imprimatur: ✠Most Rev. R.P. Fabbro, C.S.B.
                Bishop of London
                April 29, 2009

Solidarity Books
1688 County Rd. 46, R.R. 1, Woodslee, On N0R 1V0

ISBN 978-0-9737718-3-1

Printed in Canada

Library and Archives Canada Cataloguing in Publication
Ryan, Michael T. (Michael Terrance), 1926-
    Handing on the faith : a resource for Evangelization / Michael T. Ryan.
ISBN 978-0-9737718-3-1
    1. Catholic Church--Doctrines--Study and teaching. I. Title.
BX2045.I553R92 2009   230'.2   C2009-901740-7

INTRODUCTION

In his Exhortation *On Evangelization in the Modern World*, published on December 8, 1975, Pope Paul VI wrote: "There is no doubt that the effort to proclaim the gospel to the people of today, who are buoyed up by hope but at the same time often oppressed by fear and distress, is a service rendered to the Church community and also to the whole of humanity" (no. 1). It is a service because the gospel really is good news. That is why Pope John Paul II also urged us many times in his pontificate to carry out "a new evangelization."

The gospel is also good news that makes sense. For this reason, St. Peter tells us: "Always be ready to make your defence to anyone who demands from you an accounting for the hope that is in you." (*I Peter* 3:15). While it is true that faith is God's gift, so that making an act of faith requires the grace of God, the fact remains that the act of faith is not a blind leap in the dark. It is an act that fully respects our rational nature. Belief in God, belief in Jesus Christ as God in human flesh, belief in the Church as the continued presence of the risen Christ among us, all this is in complete accord with the demands of the human reason and will in their search for the true and the good. While agreeing that, "above all the gospel must be proclaimed by witness," Pope Paul VI went on to add, in the document referred to above, "nevertheless, this always remains insufficient, because the finest witness will prove ineffective in the long run if it is not explained, justified." (nos. 21, 22)

Giving instructions in the Catholic faith to individual inquirers, and in more recent years directing parish programs in the Rite of Christian Initiation of Adults (R.C.I.A.), has always been for me one of the most joyful and satisfying aspects of my priestly ministry. I have also been struck by the number of Catholics who long for an opportunity to review and deepen their knowledge of their faith, and who sometimes take part in the sessions associated with these parish programs for this reason.

It has also been my experience that pastoral ministers, and Catholic teachers, at every level of the educational process, look for resources that will confirm their own faith and will assist them in building up the faith of those they seek to lead and instruct.

For these reasons, I decided to publish this series of instructions in the Catholic faith. It is one that I have developed over the years, first in giving private instructions, and then in directing a parish R.C.I.A. program. It is my hope that parts of it, at least, will be helpful to those who are directing similar parish programs, as well as to Catholics who are looking for an orderly review of their faith, and to teachers who are seeking assistance in their great vocation of teaching and training others. It is important to have a Bible handy while reading each chapter, since the text frequently calls for consulting some particular passage and presupposes that the reader has that passage available.

The eighteen chapters presented here could provide an outline for the instructional component of a parish R.C.I.A. program that begins in the fall and aims to have candidates prepared for baptism or for reception into full communion with the Catholic Church at the Easter Vigil. Each chapter concludes with a suggestion for a video that could be helpful to those leading such a program. The video can fulfill many roles: in some cases, it fills in details that may have been missing in the oral presentation; in most cases, it serves as a summary and review of what has been covered in the chapter; and occasionally it raises some question that needs to be discussed.

A number of the chapters have appendices. These are not essential to the movement of thought from one chapter to the next and so can be ignored by those who might find them a distraction. However, they do contain supplementary material – much of it from my teaching days – that I have found to be of interest to inquirers. Other appendices grew out of questions that were raised by people attending the sessions; the answers I provided to those people may be helpful to others as well. I have left these appendices in the places where the supplementary material was originally made available or where the questions were first raised.

Those looking for a deeper study of some of the topics considered in this book may find it useful to consult my book *In the Light of Faith*, Second Edition 2008. It could be helpful especially when dealing with such issues as the mystery of evil, fundamentalism, faith and science, the papal primacy and ecumenism, the Christian life, and justice issues.

"How beautiful upon the mountains are the feet of the messenger who brings good news, who announces salvation, who says to Zion, 'Your God reigns'." (*Isaiah* 52:7). It is a special privilege and grace to carry out the work of evangelization, and to be God's vehicle for bringing his good news to people. May this book offer some measure of assistance to those who carry out this great ministry.

* * *

I am grateful to many people who helped me in putting this book into its final form: to Father Michael Prieur, professor of Moral Theology at St. Peter's Seminary, who reviewed the chapters on Reconciliation and Marriage and offered helpful suggestions; to Father John Comiskey, professor of Church History at St. Peter's, who read the historical sections in the chapter on the Church and gave me important assistance; to Father David Boutette, who reviewed the entire manuscript, for his friendship, encouragement, and wise suggestions, especially for the appendix on Natural Family Planning; to several generous people in the fields of parish ministry, teaching or communications, who read earlier versions of the entire manuscript and made valuable suggestions for improvement; finally to Mr. Ron Pickersgill, who gave me advice, and who prepared the manuscript for the printer.

CONTENTS

1. Introduction to Religion. Natural and Revealed Religion. The Bible. 1

2. Jesus. The Trinity. The Incarnation. The Redemption. 17

3. The Church. 24

4. Christ Present through the Sacraments. 37

5. The Holy Eucharist. 45

6. The Mass. 58

7. The Sacrament of Reconciliation. 67

8. The Sacrament of Matrimony. Church Law on Marriage. 76

9. The Sacrament of the Sick and the Sacrament of Holy Orders. 81

10. Mid-Point Review and Questions. Tour of the Church 92

* * *

11. The Christian Life. Part I. 96

12. The Christian Life. Part II 105

13. The Social Teaching of the Church. 119

14. Prayer. 127

15. The Devotional Life. Veneration of Mary and the Saints. 134

16. The Church in Daily Life: The Liturgical Year.
    The Sacramentals. The Precepts of the Church. 140

17. The "Last Things" – Death, Judgment, Heaven, Hell, Purgatory 147

18. The Sacrament of Confirmation. Final Review and Questions. 152

    The Journey Ahead 158

Chapter 1

RELIGION: NATURAL AND REVEALED; THE BIBLE

A sudden disaster, like an airplane crash or an earthquake, brings the personal agendas of those affected to an abrupt end. Most of us are focused on our own schedules. We feel that we live busy lives, and can become absorbed in our plans, our projects, and our dreams. Unexpected tragedies, however, strongly suggest that all of us are part of a far larger Plan than our own, and it is that Plan that will always take precedence over our own.

To put the point differently, I am suggesting that many people need to question the basic attitude that characterizes the contemporary approach to daily life, at least in the West. Instead of asking themselves whether they can, or should, make God and religion a part of their world, they need to become aware of the fact that they are already part of God's world. Our culture leads us to live almost entirely in "man's" world. We have to come to terms with the truth that we live in God's world.

Religion

Religion is fundamental to the human condition. There is no culture known to us in either past history or in our present world that does not include some form of religion. There is nothing surprising about this because all human beings ask religious questions. We find ourselves asking, "What is the purpose or meaning of life?" "What must I do to find happiness?" "Where did our universe come from and where is it going?" For this reason the majority of people have some sense that there must be a "God," a "Supreme Being," a "Great Spirit" that is responsible for all that is.

The word "religion" is probably from the Latin, *religare* which means "to tie one thing to another." If there is a God, then we are inescapably tied to him. Religion is not just some polite practice like following the rules of etiquette when we eat our meals; it is an acknowledgement of the ways in which we are "tied" to God.

We speak of two kinds of religion: natural religion and revealed religion

Natural Religion

Natural religion is any form of religion that results from what we discover just by using our natural reason. When we use our reason, we find that two roads lead people to the existence of God.

The first road involves looking at the world around us. When we think about it, we cannot help but ask, "Why is there something rather than nothing?" As we reflect on this, we realize that, if there is something existing now (as there manifestly is) then there has to be something that always existed, since nothing comes from nothing. That "being that has always existed" we call "God." Such Absolute Being cannot be less than us, but must be infinitely greater than us. Clearly, it must be a personal being, not just some impersonal force.

The second road involves looking at the world within us. We notice first that all of us have a deep sense of responsibility for ourselves, a strong feeling of self-respect. We find ourselves saying things like, "I could never do that; I wouldn't be able to face myself if I did that." How do we make sense of this strong feeling if there is not someone beyond us to whom we are accountable? Second, all of us are conscious of our failings and of the many times in our lives when we and others have acted in a sinful way. Reason strongly suggests to us that we will someday have to face a judgment of some kind. Ludwig Wittgenstein, one of the greatest philosophers of the 20th century, a man who did not belong to any particular church, was convinced that in the end we will all face some kind of judgment. He said, "If that were not the case, there would be no seriousness to life at all." So most of us, when we are honest with ourselves, are aware of God as the one to whom we are morally accountable.

These two roads to God explain the existence of many "natural religions," organized codes of belief and practice through which a culture or a society acknowledges its relation to God, its dependence on God and is accountability to God.

It is interesting to reflect how much the fact of evolution casts light on natural religion. Think of those long periods of millions of years when this earth was inhabited by mammoth animals, who roamed over marvelous landscapes filled with beautiful flowers, awesome lakes, and exotic creatures of many kinds, but no humans. What was the point of a world like this? Who in this world could look at it all and respond to the God from whom it all came? Only when evolution reached the point that humans appeared did it all fit together. For now there was, in this world, a creature who could look at it all, come to realize the God from whom it came, and then respond to that God in the name of all creation. When we pray and when we try to develop this world as we think God wants it done, we are the voice and hands through which all of nature gives thanks and praise to the God from whom it all came.

Revealed Religion

Natural religion is based simply on what we can discover using our natural reason. Revealed religion is any religion that claims to have resulted from God revealing to us certain things about God, about ourselves and about our relation to God. "Revelation" is from *revelare*, which means "lifting the veil." Think of lifting a bride's veil so we can see her face. God lifts the veil so that we may, in some limited sense, see the face of God.

Has God revealed himself to us? Avery Dulles, one of the most prominent theologians of our time, a man who is a convert to Christianity and to the Catholic Church, writes, "Reason itself suggests the probability of revelation. If there is a God, and if he created the world, he will presumably interest himself in human affairs" (*The New World of Faith*, Huntington, Indiana 2000, p. 21). To answer the question whether God has revealed himself to us in some way, however, we need to conduct an historical investigation. Are there signs we can point to that show God revealing himself to humans in some historical setting?

Three major religions say, "Yes, God has removed the veil." Judaism, Christianity, and Islam all claim that God has progressively revealed himself to us, beginning with Abraham, a desert nomad who lived about 1,850 years before Christ. "The religions of the Middle East and of the West are dominated by the conviction that God acts in history" (Dulles, *loc. cit.*). Abraham was the leader of a small tribe that numbered perhaps one hundred people. God told Abraham that he was going to make him the father of a great people, a people who would be taught and guided by God so that they could be a "light" to all other nations, a sign to all people of the reality of God and of how God wanted us to live. Why Abraham? That is hidden in the mysterious Providence of God.

God did guide the people that arose from Abraham, and revealed himself to them both by the actions he did among them and by the prophets he sent to interpret those actions for them.

God's intention, we said, was that the people of Abraham would be a light to the nations, by their life, their teachings, and their worship. Sadly, however, rather than being a light to the nations around them, they repeatedly adopted some of the bad ways of those nations and so failed in the mission God had given them. Through prophets (literally, people who "speak for" God) God tried again and again to recall his chosen people to their great vocation, but largely in vain.

Finally, the prophets began to speak of God raising up one person from among this nation who would himself fulfill the calling of his people. This person would himself be the "light" that the people as a whole had failed to be. As devout Jews looked forward to this promised one they began to refer to him as "the Anointed One." (Among the Jews, priests, prophets, and kings were all anointed with holy oil as a sign that they were God's chosen representatives). In Hebrew, an anointed one is *mashiah*, from which we get our word "Messiah." In Greek, it is *christos*, from which we get our word "Christ." People looked forward to the coming of the Messiah or the Christ.

Christians believe that promised one is Jesus. Religious Jews, who reject Jesus as the Messiah, are people who are still waiting for the Messiah to appear. Muslims are people who follow Mohammed, a Middle Eastern leader who in 622 A.D. claimed that, though Jesus was one of the prophets, he, Mohammed, was God's final prophet, called to lead people back to the original Abrahamic religion.

How do we know that this revelation dating from Abraham is truly from God? In particular, how do we know that Jesus is God's final and supreme revelation to us? These are questions about the "signs of revelation." What signs does this revelation exhibit that show its divine origin?

This is a big question to which a person could devote a great deal of study. Briefly, we can point to the following general features of this revelation. The revelation to the people of Abraham shows its divine origin, first in the message itself, which is superior in important respects to that of other ancient peoples (its monotheism, its sense of both the transcendence and the immanence of God, its moral code). Second, it shows its divine origin in the unique character of the Jewish community, which retained its belief in the one God, creator of heaven and earth, in spite of long years in exile and subjection to powerful empires.

For Christians, the signs that Jesus is indeed God's "Promised one," and God's supreme and final revelation to us, are in general the following. First, the person of Jesus is unique in history. He appears to us as all that a human could and should aspire to be, and has been an inspiration for all kinds of people in every age. His life is one of complete and balanced virtue; he combines authority and courage with meekness and humility. His attitude of total trust in the Father is joined to an utterly selfless love for people. A number of people, including the famous British writer, C.S. Lewis, and the great French Catholic theologian, Jean Danielou, have argued also from Jesus' testimony to himself. His claim to be God's supreme revelation to us marks him as a madman, a liar, or someone bearing witness to the truth. Everything we see in the life of Jesus clearly rules out the first two possibilities.

Second, there is the teaching of Jesus. His picture of God and his moral teaching in particular go far beyond what natural religion provides. St. Thomas Aquinas, the great 13th century Catholic scholar, remarks: "Not one of the philosophers before the coming of Christ, no matter how hard he struggled to do so, could learn as much about God and matters necessary for eternal life as one poor old lady can know by faith after Christ's coming."

In the third place, there are the signs that Jesus fulfills, and goes far beyond, what the Hebrew prophets had dimly foreseen as they looked forward to the coming of the Messiah. Fourth, there are the miracles of Jesus. It is impossible to eliminate these from the Gospels. The whole picture we are given of Jesus is one that only makes sense if we accept the testimony of witnesses that Jesus did perform miracles. Moreover, those miracles are not crass displays of power, such as we find in some other ancient religions. They are works of mercy, signs of a forgiving, loving, and faithful God reaching out to his people.

Next, there is Jesus' resurrection from the dead. The evidence for this is compelling. A thorough study can be found in a work by one of today's most-respected biblical scholars, the Anglican, N.T. Wright: *The Resurrection of the Son of God* (London 2003). Briefly, we can say the following. It is clear that Jesus was dead. He was killed by professional soldiers, one of whom made sure of the fact by piercing him with a spear. (*John* 19:34). It is also clear that his tomb was empty on the third day after his death; even the enemies of Christianity admitted this. Finally, the assertion by witnesses that they met the risen Christ, who was truly a bodily figure and yet also transformed, is confirmed by the amazing change in their lives, by their acceptance of an event for which nothing in their religious background had prepared them, by their faithfulness in the face of persecution, by such radical steps as changing the Sabbath from Saturday to Sunday and acknowledging Jesus as truly divine. As a final sign of the truth of Christian revelation, we can point to the Church itself, an institution that displays many signs of its divine origin; more will be said about this in future chapters.

Transmission of Revelation

If God has revealed himself to us, then it is essential that we be able to gain access to this revelation. How has this revelation, to the Jews, and then in Jesus, been handed on?

With both Jews and Christians, it was first handed on orally, through the life of the people (in its worship, traditions, life together, etc.). Thus, persons received this revelation through their engagement in the life of the people. There they continued to learn about God and to meet God.

So, it was not primarily passed on through writing. The idea of practising one's religion simply by sitting at home with one's Bible is, frankly, "unbiblical." (Keep in mind the lack of literacy in most people until about 150 years ago. Remember too that books were rare and expensive before the invention of printing by Johannes Gutenberg [1390-1468]).

It is especially the case with Christianity that revelation was at first transmitted orally. Jesus did not dictate a message to secretaries. Nor did he tell his disciples to write. Rather, Jesus founded a Church, that is, a renewed People of God. Nothing much of Jesus' life and teaching appears to have been written for about 20 years after the resurrection. The first Christian writings that became part of the New Testament are by Paul around the year 50 A.D. The first Gospel was not written until about 70 A.D. What today we call the Books of the "New Testament" were not definitively decided upon and gathered together until the fourth century. "In his *Festal Epistle* of 367, Athanasius of Alexandria provided the first full list of the twenty-seven books of the New Testament." (G. O'Collins, *Catholicism,* Oxford 2003, p. 118). Fixing the "canon" of the New Testament, that is, deciding which of the early Christian writings were inspired and so had to be included, was governed apparently by three things about a book: its apostolic origin, its orthodoxy, and its use in the liturgy.

Thus, although Jesus neither wrote nor asked his disciples to write, some things did eventually get written down, first in smaller collections and then finally in the four Gospels, the Acts of the Apostles, and the other books and letters that make up today's New Testament.

Note the qualification we make, that eventually "some" things came to be written down. This implies that not all things came to be written down. The *Gospel of John* (21:25) says as much. So it is not always the right thing to ask of a Christian teaching, "Where does it say that in the Bible?" The more important question should be, "Is this the traditional teaching of the Church that Jesus established?" We must always remember that the New Testament comes from the Church, not the other way around.

The canonical collection of sacred books, that is, the collection of books officially recognized by the Church as inspired by God, is today called the "Bible" (*Biblia Sacra* meaning "sacred books"). It is a collection of 73 books: 46 Old Testament books and 27 New Testament books. It is made up of different kinds of books, written by different people in different times, belonging to different cultures, to meet different needs. Some contain "sacred stories," some history, some prayers, others wisdom sayings, etc. The oldest parts of the Bible go back to about 950 B.C. The last book of the Bible was written somewhere around 100 A.D. What unites them all is that they were all written under God's guidance. Therefore, we have a guarantee of *the religious truths* they teach us.

How to Read the Bible

We need to ask ourselves, What kind of literature is this book or passage? What was the intention of the author? Take the example of *Genesis*. The first eleven chapters are sacred stories, intended to teach us religious truths. They give us a religious account, not a scientific one. That is why we find such statements as that the sun and moon were not created until "the fourth day." *Genesis* comes probably from three different sources, written at different times. The book received its final form during the Babylonian Captivity. The final editor was anxious to preserve the faith of the Jews during their long years in Babylon, so he stressed that all was created by God and was good and was wisely ordered; the disorder in the world comes from us. He pointed out that the sun and the moon, which were worshipped by the Babylonians, were not divine, but were created by God.

We need to beware of *Fundamentalism*. The Church's great Biblical scholars have always recognized, in one way or another, a non-literal element in the Scriptures. Today's "literalists" are reading 19th century individualistic pietism back into the biblical period.

Attitude to Bible

It is the Word of God, so revere it and read it prayerfully. It is one of the places where we meet God.

Today there is a lot of joint work on the Bible undertaken by Protestant and Catholic scholars. One major difference that still exists between them is the Catholic acceptance of what are called the Deuterocanonical Books (*Judith, Wisdom, Tobias, Sirach, Baruch, 1-2 Maccabees*, portions of *Esther* and *Daniel*). These books are present in the Septuagint (Greek) version of the Old Testament but not in the Masoretic (Hebrew) text. In his defence of the Catholic acceptance of these books, Gerald O'Collins states, "The New

Testament authors, by regularly following the Septuagint version of the scriptures, show how in general that version was the primary Bible for first-century Christians. In particular, at times the New Testament authors echo or quote deuterocanonical books and make no distinction between the authority of those books and the other scriptures they inherited from their Jewish background." (*op. cit.*, p. 122).

The English version of the Bible used by Catholics in the liturgy today is the *New Revised Standard Version* (NRSV), an ecumenical translation produced by Protestant and Catholic scholars together. This version is the one used for worship in other major Christian denominations as well. Many also use the common lectionary for Sunday readings (so that one is liable to hear the same readings used each Sunday in Catholic, Anglican, Lutheran and several other Christian churches).

Yet the Bible remains only part of the story. Catholics point to the importance also of Tradition. Some truths known primarily through Tradition are ones that are echoed or hinted at in the New Testament but not explicitly stated there. A good example is the belief in purgatory, which is reflected in the early practice of praying for the dead. The British theologian, Herbert McCabe, describes purgatory as follows: "The final detachment from the things of this world that happens to us when we die in Christ." (*The Teaching of the Catholic Church*, London 1985, p. 46). Because detachment from the things of this world is liable to be incomplete for most of us when we die there has to be an intermediate state in which this "final" detachment takes place. Praying for the dead presupposes that the prayers of the faithful can help it to come about, so the dead can then enter eternal life.

"Tradition" refers to the process of "handing on." Some of what has been authentically handed on by the Church-community is made explicit in the creed and in other Church teachings that perhaps are only implicit in Scripture.

Catholics are "People of the Book," but above all "People of the Church." For the Church produced the Bible, and not the other way around. We treasure the Bible as the Word of God, though we recognize that it is not a substitute for living as a part of God's People, and we believe that it is only within the life of that People that we have the fullest sense of what God reveals to us.

Video
> *What Catholics Believe about the Bible* (Liguori Publications)

Appendix I

PURGATORY

1. The practice of offering prayers for the dead dates from the earliest times. The custom of offering Mass for the dead may well go back to the 2nd century. By the 4th century it was common practice.

2. As a testimony of the early belief of the Church, consider these words of St. John Chrysostom, one of the most respected of early Church leaders (died 407 A.D.): "Let us help and commemorate them. If Job's sons were purified by their father's sacrifice, why would we doubt that our offerings for the dead bring them some consolation? Let us not hesitate to help those who have died and to offer prayers for them."

3. Similar witness can be found in many of the early Church teachers: Tertullian (died 225), Gregory of Nyssa (died 395), Cyprian (died 258), Ephrem (died 373), Ambrose (died 397), Augustine (died 430), Gregory the Great (died 604).

4. An early work, *The Martyrdom of Perpetua and Felicitas,* written about the year 203 (authenticated in modern times), makes clear reference to the cleansing of purgatory and to the value of prayers for those in purgatory. This work had a lot to do with the Anglican scholar, Edward Pusey, changing his mind and coming to believe in purgatory at the time of the Oxford Movement in 19th century England.

5. Purgatory was formally defined at the Council of Florence (1439) and again at Trent (1563). Many doctrines long believed and taught in the Church were never formally defined until someone seriously denied them.

Appendix II

ISLAM

Introduction

There are at least three reasons why we should learn more about Islam. First, Muslims are becoming much more numerous in Canada due to immigration. Second, radical or "fundamentalist" Muslims have been associated with recent acts of terrorism, and with anti-Catholic activity. We need to understand why this is so, and sharpen our ability to distinguish between "fundamentalists" and other Muslims. Third, Christians and Muslims need to work together for a more just and peaceful world.

1. Brief History

The name "Islam," means "surrender." Adherents of this faith are called "Muslims," meaning, "those who have surrendered (to God)." Its founder was Mohammed (570-632 A.D.), born at Mecca, in present-day Saudi Arabia. About 610, he began to claim he received a "recitation" (Qur'an) from the Angel Gabriel and the Spirit. Note the word "recitation." Muslims regard the Qu'ran as literally dictated by God, with no room for a human author. His reception of this "recitation" made him, he said, the last of the prophets, sent to restore the purity of God's religion, which he saw as beginning with Abraham (as Christians and Jews also see it). In 622, he and his followers fled to Medina. This date is usually seen as the beginning of Islam.

2. Beliefs and Practices

Islam is monotheistic: "There is no god but God (Allah), and Mohammed is his messenger." It calls on its followers to submit wholeheartedly to God's inscrutable decrees. It does not acknowledge Jesus as God (especially because it sees the Trinity as compromising belief in one God), but it does revere him as a prophet, and it honours Mary, his Virgin Mother. It also refers to angels, to various prophets and messengers, to resurrection of the body and judgment, and predestination. However, there is no original sin (it is not a doctrine emphasized in Islam, though it is acknowledged in the Qu'ran), no need for redemption, and no redeemer. There is no church, no priesthood, no sacraments, and almost no liturgy.

Islam stresses orthopraxis, or the moral life. Hence the emphasis on the "five pillars" of Islam: profession of faith in Islam, prayer (five times a day), fasting (especially during Ramadan, a month of spiritual renewal), almsgiving, and pilgrimage (hajj).

There is no central authority in Islam, a weakness that makes it possible for extreme forms of Islam to take hold. Appeal is simply to the Qu'ran, whose interpretation consequently becomes important. There is also appeal to the Sunnah, or customs of Mohammed, his oral commentaries, remarks and teachings (hence the "Sunni" Muslims), and to Islamic Law (the shari'ah). The religious and the political are closely associated within Islam.

3. Groups Within Islam

Most Muslims belong to the majority Sunni group. However there is a sizeable minority called the Shi'ite. A large percentage of the people of Iran are Shi'ites. This division goes back to the time of Mohammed, with the Shi'ites following Mohammed's cousin and son-in-law, Ali ("Followers of Ali" or "Shi'at Ali").

The mystical tradition within Islam is known as Sufism (from "sufi" = "wool," the rough clothing worn by self-denying seekers after truth). Whatever its origins (around the 8th century), it resulted in a movement among Muslims that pursues an ascetic and contemplative life, focused on the love of God.

An important later development within Islam is Wahhabism. More will be said about this below.

4. Pope John Paul's Essay on Islam

In his 1994 book, *Crossing the Threshold of Hope*, Pope John Paul has a short chapter on Islam. He refers to Vatican II's document, *Nostra Aetate*, which says: "The Church also has a high regard for the Muslims, who worship one God, living and subsistent, merciful and omnipotent, the Creator of heaven and earth." Because of their monotheism, the pope says, believers in Allah are particularly close to us.

However, the pope then goes on to point out that the Qur'an significantly reduces divine revelation. The many wonderful things God has said about himself, first through the prophets, and then through his Son, have been set aside. Though the Qur'an has some of the most beautiful names in human language for God, it is a God who is outside the world, a God who is only Majesty, never Emmanuel, God-with-us, never God who took our human nature in Jesus. Moreover, there is no idea of redemption, of the role of the cross and the Resurrection of Jesus. Hence, the anthropology of Islam is distant from that of Christianity. Still, says the pope, the religiosity of Muslims deserves respect. For example, consider their fidelity to prayer. We see them falling to their knees to immerse themselves in prayer, no matter what the time or place.

He encourages us to carry on dialogue with Muslims. In some situations, it has been an encouraging process, though Christians encounter serious difficulties in those places where a radical or fundamentalist version of Islam deprives Christians of religious freedom, and even tries to impose Islam on them. There is a Pontifical Institute of Arabic and Islamic Studies in Rome, run by the Missionaries of Africa, and an Islamic Studies Centre in Cairo, operated by the Dominicans. There are also now some groups of Christians and Muslims who meet together on a regular basis in larger cities. Many years ago when Pope Pius XI sent a new Apostolic Delegate to Libya, he reminded him: "Do not think you are going among infidels. Muslims attain to Salvation. The ways of Providence are infinite."

5. Contemporary Islamist (Radical) Movements

The events of 9/11/01 in the United States focused attention on Radical Islam, which is usually called Islamism. This is primarily a modern phenomenon. Three names are important for understanding it.

First, Muhammad ibn al-Wahhab. The main source of radical Islam today is Saudi Arabia. The modern Saudi state dates from 1926, when it acquired by conquest the Islamic Holy land of Mecca and Medina. However, the original Saudi state goes back to the 18th century when it came about as the result of an alliance between a "reformer," Muhammad ibn al-Wahhab, and a tribal chief named Muhammad al-Sa'ud.

Wahhab was born in Arabia in 1703. In the years 1737-40 he issued a call to what he termed "an original, authentic Islam." His version sees ritual as superior to intention; it permits no reverence for the dead; it forbids intercessory prayer through the Prophet or saints. It has strict rules on the times and positions of prayer. It regards Shi'ites and Sufi's as not true Muslims. It despises music (which makes us forget God!). It opposes all other religions. Public worship by non-Muslims is forbidden. It is totalitarian. Wahhabism is the official form of Islam in modern Saudi Arabia, which exports it to other countries.

Second, Sayyid Abu 'Ala Maududi (1903-79) is the intellectual father of today's radical form of Islam. An Indian Muslim radical and journalist, he was influenced by the writings of Alexis Carrel, a French surgeon and biologist, who spoke of the "corruption" of modern living. Maududi himself denounced the West as a sewer of vice and wickedness. He was also influenced by communism and fascism in the sense that he admired their power to move the masses. He also adopted the Marxist idea of the need for permanent revolution.

Third, Sayyid Qutb [KUH-tahb] (1906-1966) was an Egyptian schoolteacher who adapted the ideas of Maududi. The author of two influential books, he saw Islam as the remedy to the spiritual destitution of the West, and said that Muslims are to express their opposition to "godless activity" with their very lives.

It is important not to confuse Islamism, or radical Islam, with Islam in general. Islam has shown that it can live in peace with others. There were examples of this in the Ottoman Empire. Spain and other parts of the world saw Muslims and Christians coexisting for centuries. In today's world, Turkey, as well as Bosnia and Kosovo have been examples of such living together. Radical Islam is a modern phenomenon that owes a good deal to contemporary Western thought. It is also worth noting what a British historian has recently demonstrated: present day Islamist rhetoric about the Crusades, which portrays today's westerners as "Crusaders" intent on destroying

Islam, is largely based on faulty pictures of the Crusades promoted by the 19th century works of Joseph-Francois Michaud and Sir Walter Scott. (See Jonathan Riley-Smith, *The Crusades, Christianity and Islam* N.Y. 2008, especially Chapter 4).

Chapter 2

JESUS

Human Sin

Most people have some familiarity with the biblical story of Adam and Eve. At the very least they recall Adam claiming something like: "The woman made me do it!" It is important now, however, to read carefully the entire Chapter 3 of *Genesis*. It is a remarkable piece of literature. It is a "sacred story," one that uses figurative language to express some important religious truths. While it makes use of ancient traditions, it is above all a profound meditation on human sin. It looks at our relations with God, with one another, with ourselves, and with our world, and draws attention to the ways in which they are tied together. Indeed, it is such a wise and insightful reflection that we realize at once we should not take the picturesque details literally. The wise writer of this study of human sin was surely not a person who really thought that snakes talked!

Consider the points this chapter makes: (a) God made all things good. (b) Evil comes not from God but from human action. (c) At the beginning of human history, humans took a "wrong turning." It was a "missed opportunity." Catholic teaching is that God offered us a supernatural life and goal, an unending life of intimate friendship with God, but we lost it. The tragic character of the loss is symbolized by the figure of the angels placed at the gates of Paradise at the end of the chapter. (d) We see also the consequences of sin. Turning against God brings about a turning against one another: Adam turns against Eve, his own wife, his other self, "flesh of his flesh." The same point will be made in Chapter 4 when, after turning against God, Cain murders his own brother, Abel. Finally, this point will be made once more in Chapter 11 where, after ignoring God in their building of the Tower of Babel, nations lose the ability to communicate with one another. Turning against God also affects person's relations with their own selves; this is the significance of saying that Adam and Eve became ashamed of their nakedness. Finally, turning against God has the result that even nature, in some sense, turns against us; this is the point made when we are told that those human activities that are our glory will become painful and arduous, childbirth for Eve and human work for Adam.

So, the relationships are tied together. The rupture in our relationship with God brings about a break in our relationship with one another, in our relationship with our own self, and in our relationship with nature. What a profound meditation this is on the nature of human sin!

What this sacred story makes clear is the truth that early in our collective life we humans took a wrong direction. In turning against God, we lost what might have been, an enduring relationship of intimacy and friendship with God. This is the first meaning of the expression, "original sin," In addition, sin enters into human history; it becomes a kind of "social reality" that solicits us. This is a second meaning of "original sin." Each of us is born into a society that "invites" us to adopt selfish ways, prejudices, and various "isms." There is a sickness that afflicts all things human, a certain ambiguity. Our fallen world is like a broken mirror (Cardinal Newman's image) that reflects God's glory but distorts it. Yet human nature itself is not corrupted; it is weakened, but not corrupted.

Redemption

Read St. Paul's *Letter to the Romans* 5: 12-21.

This is not an easy passage to read, but the point it makes is clear enough. What we have here is the response to Chapter 3 of *Genesis*. This, and similar passages in St. Paul, provide the basis for the developed doctrines of original sin and redemption. (This is explained at length in Gerald O'Collins, *Catholicism,* Oxford 2003, page 160 and following). Where Adam brought about our downfall, Jesus has brought about our reconciliation. Redemption is the result of God's loving initiative. It is God who brings about reconciliation by sending his Son as one of us. Jesus, in our name, offers the Father the loving obedience and sacrifice that we, as humans, have failed to offer. In his love for us, he lets himself "be victimized by the powers of this world" (O'Collins, *op. cit.*, p. 163). It is in our free union with him that we are able to participate in this reconciliation.

Our human situation is as follows. Because of original sin, each of us is born into a state of separation from God. Our solidarity with fallen humanity involves this. We come into this world lacking God's "grace." Our need of redemption is therefore absolute. Besides that, our social situations also entice us into our own personal sins, and all of us are painfully aware of the fact that we sometimes give in to such enticement.

Redemption is offered us because of Christ. His perfect obedience to the Father is the response humanity failed to make, and that He makes in our name and on our behalf.

We enter into solidarity with Christ, and with his act of loving obedience to the Father, by being joined to his saving community, the Church. Normally this comes about through Baptism. Within that community, we find relationship with God restored. We call this restored relationship the state of "sanctifying grace." We become adopted sons and daughters of the Father (and no longer just "creatures" responding to their Creator). We also find within this saving community many enticements to a different kind of life, a life in imitation of Christ. We find there also the resources we need to combat the "sin of the world."

The Creed

At this point it is helpful for us to look at the *Apostles Creed*. This is an early statement of Christian belief dating from the 2nd or 3rd century. It is a "pre-Baptismal" creed dealing with the truths to be accepted by an adult in order to receive Baptism, so it does not treat of the "mysteries" like the Mass and the Eucharist, which were only revealed to the initiated, those already baptized into the Christian community.

The Trinity

"I believe in God the Father Almighty, creator of heaven and earth, and in Jesus Christ, his only Son, our Lord, who was conceived by the power of the Holy Spirit and born of the Virgin Mary."

These words introduce us to the doctrine of the Trinity. In the one God there are three Persons – the Father, the Son and the Holy Spirit. There is only one God, yet this God is mysteriously three Persons. How can this be?

Clearly, the intimate nature of God is infinitely beyond our understanding; that fact should not surprise us. However, we can say a few things that may be helpful.

For one thing, there is a remote preparation for this truth in the Old Testament, where God is presented as *Wisdom, Word, and Spirit.* Something else that may help us is St. Augustine's suggestion. He points out that we humans can detect within ourselves a certain duality; we can know ourselves and we can love ourselves. The suggestion is that in God that self- knowledge and self-love are distinct Persons. (cf. O'Collins, *op. cit.* p. 142).

The Incarnation

This first part of the Creed also introduces us to *the doctrine of the incarnation.* Consider the meaning of that word. The Latin word *carnis* means "flesh." Jesus is God the Son who has taken on human flesh, a human nature like our own. So Jesus is truly human and yet he is truly divine, God the Son. What a profound dignity this confers on humans; our God has taken on our human nature and become one of us. In so doing, he has identified with every single human being.

What evidence have we for this astounding truth of the incarnation? When we look at the Gospels, it is clear that, at least implicitly, Jesus claimed an authority and identity on a par with God, for example in the way he changed the Mosaic Law in his Sermon on the Mount; in the way he forgave sins; in the way he took over the Temple; in the way he spoke of relationship with himself as being essential to people's relation with God. (Cf. O'Collins, *op. cit.* p. 134).

See also the clear testimony of St. Paul, for example, the equivalently Trinitarian formula in *2 Cor.* 13:13, "The grace of the Lord Jesus Christ, the love of God, and the communion of the Holy Spirit be with all of you." This was written around the year 60 A.D., twenty years before Matthew's Gospel. At some point in the 1st century, Christian communities stopped baptizing simply "in the name of Jesus," and began baptizing in the name of the Father, the Son, and the Holy Spirit. We see this baptismal formula reflected in *Matt.* 28:19.

The great heresies (that is, erroneous attempts at understanding) during the early centuries denied either the divinity of Jesus (e.g. the Ebionites) or his humanity (e.g. the Docetists). The first seven General Councils of the Church dealt with various aspects of the Incarnation and the Trinity, and their declarations reflect a growth and deepening of the Church's understanding of these great truths. Thus (1) Nicaea (325) affirmed the divinity of Christ against Arius; (2) Constantinople I (381) affirmed the Trinity; (3) Ephesus (431) applied the title *Theotokos* that is, "Mother of God" to Mary; (4) Chalcedon (451) defined the Hypostatic Union of the human and divine natures of Christ in the one Person of God the Son; (5) Constantinople II (553) reaffirmed the Divinity of Christ; (6) Constantinople III (680/1) again defined the two natures of Christ; Nicaea II (787) dealt with the iconoclast controversy, and affirmed the legitimacy of venerating icons or images of the sacred humanity of Christ.

The Saving Death and Resurrection of Jesus

"He suffered under Pontius Pilate, was crucified, died and was buried. He descended to the dead. On the third day he rose again. He ascended into heaven and is seated at the right hand of the Father." Here is the doctrine of redemption, what was accomplished for us by the perfect obedience of Jesus.

"He will come again to judge the living and the dead." We will speak about this in a later chapter.

"I believe in the Holy Spirit." Here is reference to the Third Person of the Blessed Trinity. We will also speak more about this in one of our later chapters.

So Who is Jesus?

He is the Promised Messiah, the fulfillment of Old Testament longing and preparation.

He is God the Son, who took on our human nature. This is the most startling event in human history. No wonder we date our years from it! This is the great truth of our faith.

He is the Redeemer. By his passion, death and resurrection he opens to us the way to eternal life. (Cf. O'Collins, *op.cit.* p. 160-164)

Video

 What Catholics Believe about Jesus Christ. (Liguori)

Appendix

THE ORIGIN OF SIN IN CHAPTER 3 OF GENESIS

If God made all things good, how could human beings ever have sinned and so brought about evil? Several things might be said about this.

First, God made human beings free. Humans have intelligence and will and so have freedom of choice. It is at once our glory and our danger. Having made us free, God respects our use of freedom, even when we choose badly. The point made in the Biblical story is that evil originates with human action, not with God.

Second, it is true, however, that the story in Chapter 3 of *Genesis* does not give us an ultimate explanation for the origin of evil, nor does it claim to be doing so. No motive is given, for example, for the serpent's action in tempting Adam and Eve. The narrator is clearly leaving this issue open; it is a riddle, a mystery.

Third, the fact remains that God could have prevented humans from sinning without interfering with their freedom. As the British theologian, Herbert McCabe, points out: "Freedom does not mean independence of God. It means independence of other creatures." (*God Matters*, Springfield, Ill. 1991, p. 37). We are left in the end with the conclusion that, though we can suggest reasons why a good God could allow evil, and especially moral evil, to exist, the presence of evil in the world is for us, ultimately, a mystery. For an extended treatment of this question, see Michael Ryan, *In the Light of Faith* Second Edition, Woodslee 2008, Chapter 2)

Chapter 3

✳ THE CHURCH

Who is Jesus? He is no mere religious preacher. He is God, who came among us and shared our human nature. What an astounding truth this is! Clearly, it is supremely important for us to know what he did and what he taught us. Yet this event took place 2000 years ago and Jesus has long since ascended to the Father. So how do we make contact today with what he said and did? We might reply that we can and should read what Jesus told us in the New Testament. But is this our only contact with the greatest event in human history?

The question we need to ask is, What provision did Jesus himself make for those of us who would live in succeeding centuries? Here we should read the Apostles Creed again. This time we take it up to the phrases, *"I believe in the Holy Spirit, the holy Catholic Church ...."* Note the link between the Holy Spirit and the Church. What do we mean here by Church? This is a crucial question.

✳ Pentecost

Read *The Acts of the Apostles*, 1:1-5 and 2:1-18

Pentecost is the Jewish feast that occurs 50 days after Passover (and so for Christians 50 days after Easter). Though the feast had various meanings, it may well have been a feast on which the Israelites celebrated the renewal of their covenant with God.

St. Luke writes about the Christian event of Pentecost in colourful language; there is a violent wind and there are tongues of fire. It is meant to recall the fire and wind that accompanied God's presentation of the Law to Moses on Mount Sinai in the book of *Exodus*. That event established God's covenant with the People of Israel, the People of God. What we witness here in the Book of *Acts* is the new or renewed covenant that God is making with the new or renewed People of God.

The Holy Spirit is the great gift of the final age. The Spirit who descended on Jesus at his baptism by John now descends on Jesus' community, the Christian Church. The Spirit joins the Christian community to the Risen

Christ. The Spirit thereby transforms the Church from a mere organization of people into a living reality. The Spirit is referred to as the soul of the Church, the source of its life. The Church is a human community (sometimes painfully so) but, thanks to the Spirit's presence within it, it is also a divine community.

Note also that the people from various nations listening to the preaching of the disciples all understand them in their own language. The Spirit (and therefore also the Church) is a source of unity to people. This scene is the reversal of what happened at the Tower of Babel in Chapter 11 of *Genesis* when people, ignoring God, became incapable of understanding one another and so became divided from one another.

The Church as the People of God

The Church is called in Greek the *ekklesia* which is literally "the people God has called together." Because of the presence of the Holy Spirit within this people, the Church is a living community that makes Christ present to the world. Jesus' ascension into heaven does not mean that he has left us. Rather, as he himself said, he ascended so that he could send the Holy Spirit on his people and so be present in the world in a new and powerful way through this Church-community. Therefore, the Church makes Christ present. For example, it makes present to us:
- his teaching
- his healing presence in the Sacraments
- his care of the poor and the sick
- his holiness (the saints)
- his miracles (e.g. Lourdes)

Because it is the Holy Spirit that makes the Church to be the presence of Christ in the world, this is a guaranteed or infallible presence. The Church unfailingly makes Christ present, and can be counted on to give us his teaching without error.

The Church as the Body of Christ

Read *I Corinthians* 12:12-22. Consider the ancient physiology behind this image. The people of St. Luke's and St. Paul's day saw the head as the source of life and activity in a person. The head is joined to the body by the spirit. Through the spirit, the head thus accomplishes its purposes through the various members of the body. In St. Paul's application, the Head is Christ. The Holy Spirit joins the body (that is, us, the Church-community) to Christ. Hence, Christ is present and active in the world through the Church-community.

Notice too how St. Paul stresses the importance of the various organs for different purposes. Every member of the Church-community is an organ, and so has a role, a part, in making Christ present and active in the world.

It is thus the whole Church-community that makes Christ present. So it is within the Church-community that we find and encounter Christ. Notice that St. Paul did not go around converting individuals; he went about founding (local) churches.

The Church as the Fundamental Sacrament

We will explore this notion further in our next chapter. But we just note here that the Church-community is referred to as the "sacramental" presence of Christ in the world.

Where is the Church of Christ?

Read *Matthew* 28:16-20. Here is Jesus' guarantee. He promises that his Church will be his continued presence until the end of the world. That means the Church Jesus established is still here in the world. So where are we to find it?

This is the same question as asking: Who are the Church of Christ? Who make it up? We answer that question as follows.

First, it is Baptism that joins us to Christ and therefore makes us part of his Church-community. In some real sense, all the baptized are part of the Church-community. If we are joined to Christ we are somehow joined to his Church-community, his People. This is an important consideration for ecumenical relations and action among Christians. It is referred to in number 3 of Vatican II's *Decree on Ecumenism* and in number 15 of its *Dogmatic Constitution on the Church.*

26

Secondly, two other conditions must be fulfilled for *full* belonging or full incorporation into the Church. One of those conditions is that we must accept all that Jesus taught, not just parts of it. This condition seems obvious. If we are Jesus' disciples then we have to let ourselves be taught by him (and so by his Church).

The other condition required is that we must accept, and be in union with, the authority that Jesus established in his Church. For Jesus did indeed establish an official leadership or authority in his Church. It was not just an amorphous group of followers that he gathered around him. It is clear that the 12 apostles, for example, represented an official leadership. They were the 12 Patriarchs of the new or renewed People of God, just as there had been 12 Patriarchs in God's original People.

[Some 20th century scholars deny this organized character of the Church that Jesus established. They speak of "early Catholicism" in the New Testament, and portray it as a loss of the original vision. But a careful examination of the New Testament evidence shows there was an established form of authority in the Church from the beginning, and that this developed into the three-fold ministry of Bishop, Priests and Deacons by the beginning of the second century. (Cf. O'Collins, *op. cit.,* p. 8-12)]

Among the apostles, Peter had a special place. Thus see *Matthew* 16:13-19: "And I tell you, you are Peter, and on this rock I will build my church, and the gates of Hades will not prevail against it." This disciple's name was Simon. Jesus here changes his name to "Peter." This was not a name used by people at that time; it was a word that meant "rock." Jesus gives Simon a name that signifies the role he is giving him in his Church. He is to be the rock, the centre of unity and stability in the Church. It is as if I was the owner of a bank and I established a second location for my bank. Then I made you manager of that second location by saying: "You are branch, and to this branch I entrust my new bank."

Now see *Luke* 22: 31-34: "Simon, Simon, listen! Satan has demanded to sift all of you like wheat, but I have prayed for you that your own faith may not fail; and you, when once you have turned back, strengthen your brothers." Peter is going to deny Christ during the passion, but he is also going to repent and he must then be the source of unity and strength to the others.

Finally look at *John* 21:15-17. In this passage the Risen Jesus asks Peter three times if he loves him. When Peter replies "yes," Jesus tells him to "Feed my lambs," "tend my sheep," "feed my sheep." Jesus here confers on Peter the role of leadership he had earlier promised.

There are also many other passages in the Gospels that show Peter's role of leadership. Finally, in the *Acts of the Apostles* this role of leadership is obviously taken up by Peter in the early Church.

Peter will eventually end up in Rome and it is there he was crucified. Since the role of leadership given to him became not less important but even more important as the Church grew, Christians came to see Peter's successor in the Church of Rome as carrying on that role of leadership. It should be noted that no other early Church lays claim to being the location of Peter's successor; it is acknowledged by all to be Rome.

So Peter's successor today is the Bishop of Rome, the man we call the Pope. The Pope is the centre of unity for the Church. Full belonging to the Church involves acceptance of the primacy of Peter and so of the Pope, his successor. Pope Benedict XVI is the 262nd successor of Peter.

All of this was largely accepted by most Christians for the first thousand years of Christianity. What happened then? Two painful divisions took place: a permanent break between Eastern and Western Christianity that gradually took shape between the 5th and the 13th centuries, and several breaks within Western Christianity in the 16th century.

The Break Between Eastern and Western Christianity

The first event was The East-West Schism. This is the unfortunate break between Eastern and Western Christianity that unfolded over a period extending from the 5th to the 13th century, with political, cultural and doctrinal issues as a backdrop to several key events. East and West had, early on, developed some differences in liturgy and in disciplinary matters that made Eastern and Western Christianity distinctive but they were united as one Church in one faith until the definitive break at the time of the 4th crusade.

Three theological issues were (and are) involved in the debate between

East and West: (1) the addition of *filioque* to the Creed by the West ("the Holy Spirit proceeds from the Father *and* the Son" rather than just from the Father); (2) the use of unleavened bread in the Eucharist by the West; (3) the precise nature of the papal primacy.

Behind the scenes however were political and cultural factors. Politically the West became increasingly occupied with coming to terms with the Barbarian invasions, while the East was engaged in a struggle with Islam. The West achieved a measure of political stability when Pope Leo III crowned Charlemagne Emperor of the West in Rome on Christmas Day in the year 800. In effect, this brought about a political separation from Constantinople.

When the Bulgarians accepted Christianity during the papacy of Nicholas I (856-67) there was a battle over whether they would follow the Eastern or Western liturgy. Photius, the Patriarch of Constantinople at the time, decided to raise the three theological issues mentioned above and caused a temporary break between Eastern and Western Christianity but unity was eventually restored, though the theological issues remained as irritants. In 1054 Michael Cerularius, Patriarch of Constantinople used them as grounds for another quarrel with Rome; this resulted in both East and West excommunicating a number of people on the other side.

The "final straw" was the 4th Crusade in the early 13th century when the Crusaders sacked Constantinople. This had not been intended by the pope but it became a major source of grievance between East and West and the basis for a total break between them. In 1274 at the Council of Lyons, reunion between Eastern and Western Christianity was achieved, but it was never accepted by everyone and it soon fell apart. At the Council of Florence (1438-39), political factors induced both East and West once again to seek unity. They did achieve agreement on their theological differences, but once again, the union was short-lived. Some Eastern Christian groups stayed in union with the Pope (and today make up a number of Eastern Rites in the Catholic Church) but most drifted away from union once again. The situation is complicated also by the fact that the Orthodox Churches are mainly national Churches enjoying a large measure of autonomy from one another.

In 1965, Paul VI and Patriarch Athenagoras of Constantinople lifted the mutual excommunications that had been imposed in 1054. Full reunion with the Orthodox was Pope John Paul II's dream, and he devoted much energy to it. Pope Benedict has indicated he is also fully committed to it.

The Protestant Reformation

The main breaks within Western Christianity occurred in the 16th century. The principal leaders in these breaks with the Catholic Church were Martin Luther in 1521, Jean Calvin in 1534, and Henry VIII in 1534. (Others included Ulrich Zwingli and John Knox).

The causes of the Protestant Reformation fall mainly into the following three categories:

First, abuses in the life of the Church. Hence, there was a need for serious reform in the Church.

Second, several dissenting ideas in theology, rooted to some extent in bad philosophy. Thus there were novel ideas in circulation and these contributed to some of the positions taken by the Protestant Reformers.

Third, the action of political leaders seeking their own interests. The stand taken by some secular rulers at critical junctures had much to do with the success of the Reformation.

First, Abuses in Church Life; the Need for Reform

In large parts of the Church – though not in all – many of the spiritual leaders, bishops and priests, lived worldly and sinful lives and provided little in the way of instruction and guidance to the faithful. To some extent, this was the result of poor training, at least of the lower clergy. In some instances, it also reflected the influence of the Renaissance, which often bred a spirit of worldliness. However, it was also the effect of secular rulers largely controlling appointments to high office in the Church. Bishops, Abbots, even Cardinals at times, were often the friends and protégés of political rulers, people unsuited to their spiritual role. Situations even arose in which Cardinals could be enemies of the Holy See.

The Renaissance was also reflected in the worldly life of several of the popes. In addition, the popes lived at Avignon in France for 68 years (1309-1377), a situation that could give the appearance of the pope being controlled by that nation. When the popes finally left Avignon and returned to Rome, a rival pope was set up at Avignon. The situation of two rival popes, one at Rome and one at Avignon, continued for forty years, from 1378 until 1417. In 1409, some people tried to put an end to it by appointing a third pope. Finally, the situation was ended in 1417 with the election of Pope Martin V, but in the intervening years great damage had been done to papal authority.

Nonetheless, there was a strong movement for reform within the Catholic Church. During the 16th century, major religious reform took place in Spain and Italy under Catholic auspices. Erasmus and other leading figures in the Church, including several great saints, also worked hard for thorough reform of the Church. Yet the leadership from Rome was not adequate to the task.

Second, Dissenting Ideas in Theology, Often Associated with Bad Philosophy

The great philosophical work of people like St. Albert the Great and especially St. Thomas Aquinas in the 13th century was gradually replaced in the 14th and 15th centuries by the views of the Franciscans John Duns Scotus and William of Ockham (1285-1347). The influence of these two men appeared especially in several widespread ideas.

First, for Ockham, universal terms, like humans or trees, that is, terms we usually speak of as naming species or genus, do not name anything in the real world but are simply creations of the human mind, based on resemblances among individuals. This is sometimes called Nominalism, but it is more accurately referred to as Conceptualism. One consequence of this view is that it prevents us from making universal statements about the real world. This leads to the death of Metaphysics and so to the view that there is not much human reason can know with certitude, including the existence of God. The truths of religion become purely a matter of faith.

Second, this involves also a loss of the idea of the Church; what we call the Church exists only in its individual members.

Third, this philosophical viewpoint leads to a strong emphasis on subjectivity, will, and freedom, a preoccupation with the thinking subject rather than with things.

Fourth, especially with Gabriel Biel (1420-1495), a German follower of

Ockham, no distinction can be drawn between Intellect and Will in God. So with him and others of this period there is increasing emphasis on God as the Supreme Will rather than God as the Supreme Wisdom; the effects of God are seen not in the created natures of things (including human nature) but in what God decrees in each situation.

There was an overall distrust of philosophy, and, since philosophy provides the framework and language in which theology is done, a suspicion of much theology as well. Some mystics called theology an obstacle to holiness.

In theology, Ockham's position led to an extrinsic theory of justification: Humans are not transformed by God's grace; they are justified because God decrees it. Their good actions remain purely natural ones, though those natural actions, he claims, can contribute to our salvation. Ockham and others also promoted a democratic theory of the Church, questioning the place of the papacy, while some views made the pope subject to a General Council of the Church. (Ockham was eventually excommunicated and carried on a polemic against the pope until his death).

Both at Erfurt University where Luther studied, and at the University of Wittenberg where he taught, the influence of Nominalism, especially as presented by Biel, was strong. Luther was partly formed by these ideas, even while later reacting against some of them.

Third, the Action of Political Leaders, Seeking Their Own Interests

First, from the time of Pope Gregory VII there had been an exaggerated view of papal power in which it was claimed that the pope had direct authority even over secular matters, with the right to depose civil rulers. This led to an attitude of bitterness toward the papacy on the part of some secular rulers. Such an attitude would lead some of them to side with the Reformers for their own political reasons.

Second, the Reformation involved, in many cases, seizure of Church lands by the secular power. This was clearly a motive for some secular leaders to join the revolt. In England, the seizure of the monasteries was an important consideration for Henry VIII, since it brought much-needed funds into the Royal Treasury.

Third, other secular motives were also involved. "For once the battle was joined – the first purely theological battle – men prepared to take part in it who were moved by impulses and desires that were not theological at all. The political ambitions of the princes; their international rivalry; the social feuds of the nobility; the interests of the bankers, traders, and the new industrialists … all these would play a highly important part in the long fight." Philip Hughes, *A Popular History of the Reformation* (Garden City, NY 1957) p. 13.

Fourth, the protection Luther received from the Elector Frederick, something unprecedented in a Church trial concerning heresy, may well have been the step that made Luther's movement something permanent.

Fifth, the Reformation in England was different from the Continental one. Henry VIII had written a treatise against Luther, defending Catholic teaching, in 1522. In recognition of this the pope conferred on him, and on his successors in perpetuity, the title "Defender of the Faith" (British monarchs still use it). Yet when, later on, Henry wanted a declaration of nullity to free him from his wife, Catherine of Aragon and was told he did not have valid grounds for one, he declared himself Head of the Catholic Church in England and granted it to himself. Henry did not himself deny the Catholic faith. His motives were his marriage and his concern for a male heir. After his break with Rome, people in England who had been won over to Reformation ideas gradually brought about a change of the faith in England.

The Catholic Church in England was in fairly good shape at the time, and most people resisted the Reformers. It took a good 50 years of official repression to put an end to the offering of Mass in England. The contemporary British historian, Eamon Duffy has demonstrated this in detail in his groundbreaking study, *The Stripping of the Altars*.

The Catholic Reform

True reform of the Church was finally officially accomplished with the Council of Trent 1545-1563. This Council did important work, not least in establishing seminaries for the training of priests.

We should not, however, lose sight of the fact that Trent solidified reforms that had already been underway for a long time in the Catholic Church, some of them well before Martin Luther. In the midst of all the corruption and failures of leadership, there were grassroots movements of renewal that bore all the signs of coming from the Holy Spirit. One can point, for example, to the establishment of the Oratory of Divine Love in Italy in 1513 under Gian Matteo Ghiberti, bishop of Verona. There was also the foundation of the Theatines, a new kind of religious order of priests, neither monks nor friars, bound by vows, observing extraordinary poverty, yet devoted to ordinary pastoral ministry; they were established in 1524 by Cajetan of Verona. We should mention as well the renewal movements in the Franciscans and the Discalced Carmelites in 1526; the establishment of the Ursuline Sisters by Angela Merici in 1535; and the foundation of the Jesuits by Ignatius Loyola in 1543.

Conclusion

Whatever the weaknesses of the Church (since it is human as well as divine) it is still that Church established by Christ, with Peter and his successors at the head, that is to endure until the end of the world. Separating oneself from the unity of this Church led by the Pope, can never be justified. Ann Widdecombe, a member of the British Parliament, who became a Catholic in 1993, stated in a 1996 interview: "When, three years ago, I crossed the bridge between the Anglican and Catholic Communions people used to ask what it was I had found with Rome that I could not have found in the Church of England, and to this question I invariably replied 'Peter'. It was one of the first real breakthroughs in my discussions with Michael Seed, the priest with the unenviable task of stripping away years of resistance to Rome and most things Roman, when he asked simply 'Where is Peter?'"

Video

What Catholics Believe About the Church (Liguori)

Appendix

HOW COULD LUTHER ABANDON THE CHURCH THAT CHRIST GUARANTEED UNTIL THE END OF THE WORLD?

There has been a great deal of research into the life and writings of Martin Luther. One thing it makes clear is that there are no easy or simple answers to this question. However, there are several things on which most scholars seem to agree, and which can be of some help in dealing with this matter.

First, Luther was, by nature, introspective and inclined to melancholy. He also felt an intense need to be certain about his salvation; he was tormented by the thought of damnation. On top of that, his decision to enter the monastery was not made in the best of circumstances. During a violent thunderstorm, he was knocked to the ground by a bolt of lightning. In his panic, he promised that if he were spared, he would enter a monastery. After he was admitted to the Augustinians in Erfurt, a community that followed a strict rule of life, he thought he would find peace.

At first, he did find some spiritual peace, but soon he was again filled with the fear of losing his soul. His training in nominalist theology led him to believe that he could merit salvation by his good works. Yet nothing he did, including frequent confession and prayers seemed to help. He found himself struggling against temptation. Even the good he did seemed to be spoiled by feelings of complacency. He felt powerless to do anything good. He was on the brink of despair.

Then in the years between 1512 and 1519, his study of St. Paul led him to a new view of justification. He came to the view that the only way one can be justified is by faith, that is, by the merits of Christ being imputed to him. Religious observance, various forms of good works had nothing to do with this; they did nothing to bring justification. It was this insight that brought him the assurance of his own salvation that he had always sought.

Luther took the position that human nature is completely corrupt. The human will is in a state of total slavery. No good work can save us. Only through faith can we be saved. This faith reinstates the sinner precisely as sinner; it does not involve an objective change in the sinner.

We can understand, then, Luther's reaction when the preacher arrived to promote the indulgence that could be granted in return for the good work of donating to the building of St. Peter's in Rome, especially when it was promoted recklessly.

"Thus Luther made an extremely personal experience the center of a new theory of salvation that was no longer in harmony with the one traditionally taught by the Church." (J.P. Dolan, *The New Catholic Encyclopedia*, Vol. 8, p. 1087)

There is also a second consideration: the influence of the humanist movement.

After Luther, in 1517, posted his theses challenging others to a debate on the doctrine of indulgences, and after his disputation with Eck in 1519, when he denied the primacy of the Pope, "Luther was the object of considerable admiration in humanist circles, being 'productively misunderstood' as sharing the humanist concern for the institutional and moral reform of the Church … Recent scholarship has drawn attention to the way in which the humanist movement expanded what was initially little more than an academic debate into an international *cause célèbre*." (F.L. Cross and E.A, Livingstone, *The Oxford Dictionary of the Christian Church,* Oxford 1997, p. 1008)

Chapter 4

CHRIST PRESENT AMONG US THROUGH THE SACRAMENTS

The Church as Sacrament

Evangelical churches today hold a strong attraction for many people. Perhaps one of the biggest reasons for that is their emphasis on a personal relationship with Christ. Many people fail to experience this relationship in the Catholic Church because they look on the sacraments as "things" or "formalities." They fail to understand that the sacraments are intimate, personal meetings with Christ. Hence the importance of this present chapter, which concentrates on the meaning of sacramentality.

In our last chapter, we considered the important truth that the Church-community is not just a purely human organization. The Holy Spirit, sent on the Church at Pentecost, lives within this community and joins it to the Risen Christ. For this reason, the Church is the Body of Christ; it is the presence and activity of Jesus Christ among us. Jesus had told his disciples that he would do even greater works through his Church than he had done during his public life: "Very truly, I tell you, the one who believes in me will also do the works that I do and in fact, will do greater works than these, because I am going to the Father." (*John* 14:12). The Church is the powerful presence and action of the Risen Christ in the world.

Hence, the official acts of the Church are the acts of Christ. We call those official acts the sacraments. In them, we meet Christ. The sacraments are symbolic acts that actually bring about what they symbolize. For example, baptism, which is an immersing in water or washing with water, actually "cleanses" us from sin. We have an intimation of this even in some natural symbols. For example, consider how a handshake, which is a sign of friendship, often actually helps to create a friendship. In the sacraments, however, the symbolic act always accomplishes what it symbolizes because it is the action of Christ.

The priest, who is the minister of most of the sacraments, is an instrumental cause of what the sacrament accomplishes. It is always Christ who is the principal cause. Think of an artist painting a scene on a canvas; the brush is the instrumental cause of the effect, but the artist is the principal cause of the effect. At the words of consecration at Mass, we might say that the priest gives a "voice" to Christ, but it is Christ who brings about the change in the bread and wine.

Hence, the sacraments do not depend for their validity or effectiveness on the holiness or worthiness of the priest or the minister of the sacrament. Who baptizes me or who offers the Mass in which I take part, for example, should be only a secondary concern for me.

The Meaning of Sacrament

The Latin word *sacramentum*, which gives us our English word, "sacrament," is actually the equivalent of the Greek word *mysterion* (or "mystery") that appears many times in the Bible. Originally, *mysterion* or "mystery" meant, in a secular context, "the secret in the mind of the king," or the "plan in the king's mind." The point is that the mystery was something hidden, yet important. If we think of the ancient world, in which the king was all-powerful, to know the king's secret or plan could be important, because he might be planning to lop off my head!

In the Old Testament, "mystery" came to mean "the plan in the mind of God, or God's plan for the salvation of human beings." This plan is hidden from us. Gradually, though, God begins to make some parts of the plan visible to us, through the prophets and through the actions that he carries out among his People, the Israelites. As time goes on, that Plan becomes more visible as it begins to point to the One whom God is going to send, the Messiah. The Plan becomes most visible in Jesus, who is the great fulfillment of the Plan. So it is Jesus who is, above all, the "mystery," or, in Latin, it is Jesus who is the "sacrament."

Note again what this means: God's Plan for our salvation is visible and present to us in Jesus. Yet it is not totally visible. It is still partly hidden because to accept Jesus for who he really is requires faith on our part; all we actually see is a man. Only when Jesus comes again in glory will the plan be totally visible and present to us.

The Church, in turn, is the sacrament of Christ. The Church makes Jesus Christ present and visible to us. The Church is the presence and activity of the Risen Lord among us, a presence and activity that are more powerful and effective than was the presence even of Jesus on the streets of Nazareth and Jerusalem.

The sacraments, which are the official acts of the church, are in turn the actions of Jesus Christ among us. The sacraments make Jesus visible and present to us in a powerful and effective way. Each sacrament is a powerful meeting that we have with Jesus Christ. A sacrament is not just a thing; it is a loving encounter or meeting with the Risen Lord.

The Church and the sacraments make Jesus (and therefore God's Plan) visible and present to us, but not yet completely. They still point beyond themselves to the full revelation of God's Plan in the Kingdom of Heaven.

To summarize what we have seen so far: A sacrament (in the wide sense) is a visible sign of something invisible. My visible gift to you is a sign of my invisible love for you. When I meet you and give you a gift, it shows my love. So too Jesus lives among us in the Church-community (cf. *Matt.* 28:18-20; *Acts* 2: 1-4) and meets us to give us visible signs of what he is doing for us invisibly. However, in the case of the sacraments the signs actually bring about what they signify.

The Seven Sacraments

Why are there *seven* sacraments? It is Jesus coming to meet us at the seven crucial points in life, or to meet the seven basic needs of life. Thus:
- Birth = Baptism, the beginning of (Christian) life
- Maturity = Confirmation
- Food = Eucharist
- Forgiveness = Reconciliation or Penance
- Marriage = Matrimony
- Leadership = Holy Orders
- Sickness and death = Sacrament of the Sick

Better still, there are:
- three sacraments of initiation: Baptism, Confirmation, Eucharist

• two sacraments of the sick: Penance and Anointing of Sick
• two sacraments of community life: Matrimony and Holy Orders

Each of the sacraments consists of a "matter" and a "form," that is, a symbolic act and a form of words. The words are officially the words of the Church, though they tend to reflect in some ways words from the Bible.

The Sacrament of Baptism

Read *Matthew* 28:19-20: these words reflect the form in which baptism was being administered in the Church at the time of Matthew's Gospel (about 80 A.D.)

The word "baptism" means "plunging" or "immersion" in water. The person goes down into the water and so is buried with Christ. The person rises from the water and so rises with Christ. Baptism joins us to Jesus in his passion, death, and resurrection. In the Catholic Church, as in many other Christian Churches, baptism by immersion is the preferred manner of baptizing, though it can also be done by pouring water on the person's head. Tradition coming from the early church tells us that baptism was administered both by immersion and by pouring water on the head, and there is some evidence in the New Testament that both manners of baptizing were used there. The words used by the one who pours the water or immerses the person are, "I baptize you in the name of the Father and of the Son and of the Holy Spirit."

Baptism literally makes us one person with Christ; it identifies us with him.

It also removes all sin from us, both original sin and (in the case of a person who has reached the age of reason) any actual sins we may have committed, so long as we are truly sorry for them. It brings about a real internal change in us. Joined to Jesus, the Son, we become adopted sons and daughters of our heavenly Father. "See what love the Father has given us, that we should be called children of God; and that is what we are." (*I John 3:1*). We become a child of the Father (no longer just a creature). This means we become capable of true friendship with God. Think what this means. Suppose your dog could be raised to your level of life so that you could discuss philosophy with him. Much more does God do to us when we are raised to a whole new level of life in Baptism, and receive in a real sense a share in God's own life.

We call that share in God's life by the name of "sanctifying grace." The Father, Son, and Holy Spirit transform us inwardly, so that the Holy Trinity can be present within us in an intimate way. God lives within us as the object of friendship. This is why serious sin is such a tragedy for us because it means we lose this intimate presence of God to us.

Baptism also makes us part of God's People. We are joined to the rest of the baptized as brothers and sisters. We are made part of that People that is called to be "a light to the nations."

We can see then why the Christian life implies a call to imitate Christ. We have been made adopted brothers and sisters of Jesus, so our vocation is to live like him. "Become what you are!" is the New Testament rule of morality, which we see repeated many times in the New Testament Letters.

Baptism is necessary for us if we are aware of that necessity. However, we also speak of baptism of desire, a situation in which a person, unaware of the necessity of baptism, still receives God's sanctifying grace by virtue of their desire – followed through in their life – to do all that God wishes them to do for salvation. We speak too of baptism of blood – a situation in which a person receives God's sanctifying grace by virtue of laying down their life in pursuit of God's will as they know it.

This raises the whole issue of the ancient teaching, "outside the Church no salvation." This is a true statement, and it can be explained as follows. All people are offered by God sufficient grace for salvation. All that grace comes through Christ, who is the one mediator. Since union with Christ means union with the Church, that means all grace comes, in some sense, through the Church. How can this be? Well, we can see the Church as having a kind of incomplete or partial presence in other religions, or even in some "secular" realities. Wherever God's grace is at work in people it tends to take on a visible and social form that has "ecclesial" or "church-like" features. Good missionaries know they will already find some sort of "presence" of the Church in other religions and in some cultural practices; it may well be mixed with ambiguous elements but it can serve as a starting-point for the preaching of the Gospel. Here it is important to read over carefully Vatican II's *Constitution on the Church*, nos. 14, 15, 16, 17.

The bishop, priest, and deacon are the ordinary ministers of Baptism. However, in a case of necessity anyone can baptize, so long as they do it correctly, and intend to do what the Church does when it baptizes.

Baptism is the doorway to the other sacraments. It can be received only once. It marks us permanently as a son or daughter of the Father, and will be our glory in heaven or our shame in hell.

Suppose someone is baptized in another Christian Church? If it is genuine baptism, then you do not baptize again if they become Catholic. Suppose a sinful person baptizes you. That does not matter; Christ is the primary cause.

Some people raise questions about infant baptism. How can you baptize a baby? It does not know what is going on. The crucial point, however, is that baptism is primarily something God does to us rather than something we do.

Video
   What Catholics Believe about Baptism (Liguori)

Appendix

THE EFFECTS OF BAPTISM

Birth	Baptism
Makes us part of *human* community	Makes us part of *Church*-community
Consequences	*Consequences*
• Separated from God's friendship	• State of friendship with God
• Many enticements to evil	• Many enticements to goodness

1. The Forgiveness of Sin:

(1) In adults, Baptism brings with it the removal of all the *personal* sins they have committed. Of course, adults need to be truly sorry for these sins, seeing them as a personal offense against God their only true Good, in order to receive forgiveness.

(2) In both adults and infants, Baptism also brings the removal of *original sin*. What does this mean? It means that the person's incapacity for relating to God – an incapacity we inherit by being part of the human race that rejected obedience to God early in human history – is overcome. One way of understanding this is to say that Baptism brings us into solidarity with Jesus Christ and his community of people, and this solidarity removes the incapacity resulting from our solidarity with the human race.

(3) Both adults and infants however still face the consequences of a human nature weakened by sin. One way of understanding this is to say that they still inherit and inhabit a world that seduces or solicits them into sinful ways of acting.

(4) All the same, the baptized find in their new Christian community the special helps Jesus provides for living a truly human and truly good life. They also find there a community of people whose way of life draws and encourages them into good ways.

2. New Life in Christ

(1) Joined to Jesus in his passion, death, and resurrection, the baptized are made the adopted brothers and sisters of Jesus and so also the adopted sons and daughters of the Heavenly Father.

(2) Union with Christ also brings the baptized a new kind of life. They are raised to a whole new level of life so that they become capable of true friendship with God rather than just being God's creatures. They share in a genuine sense, then, in the life of God. The theological term for this is sanctifying grace.

(3) The consequence of this new life of grace is that God, the Father, Son and Holy Spirit, is intimately present to the baptized person. (This presence is lost by serious sin, but can be restored by the Sacrament of Reconciliation).

(4) Sharing in the Sonship of Christ means also sharing in his inheritance – the right to eternal life with God, so long as one does not die in a state of serious sin.

3. Membership in the Church-Community

(1) To belong to Christ means to be part of his Renewed People, the Body of Christ, in which each baptized person has their own special gifts from God for the good of the whole.

(2) Membership in the Church-community also brings with it the right to the other sacraments in which we meet Christ as he strengthens us and supports us along the journey of life. It also brings us his guidance through the Church's official teaching office. It brings us his healing and strengthening presence, which is found in the entire life of the Church-community.

Chapter 5

THE EUCHARIST

The four Gospels conclude with accounts of the various appearances of the risen Lord to his disciples. Those disciples had seen him suffer and die. Now they met him in his risen and glorified humanity. Their excitement and joy are especially evident in one of the scenes in John's Gospel. Peter and the Beloved Disciple are out fishing in the lake when the Beloved Disciple sees the risen Jesus on the shore and shouts out: "It is the Lord." Peter at once jumps out of the boat and rushes through the water to Jesus (*John* 21: 1-8). We meet that same risen and glorified Lord, just as truly, when he comes to us under the sign of food in the Eucharist. With good reason, we too can cry out: "It is the Lord!"

Near the end of St. Luke's Gospel (24: 13-35) the disciples on the road to Emmaus meet the risen Lord but at first do not recognize him. When they stop to eat, we are told that he took bread, blessed it, broke it and gave it to them. Then, we are told, their eyes were opened and they knew who he was, as he vanished from their sight. When they excitedly returned to Jerusalem and reported this to the others, they told how they had recognized him "in the breaking of the bread." The early Church used this expression for the Eucharist. There we too have the privilege of recognizing the Lord in the "breaking of the bread."

We believe that we truly meet Jesus Christ in the Eucharist. Catholic teaching is that the Eucharist is not just a sign of Jesus, or a reminder of him, or a symbol of him, but the real, genuine presence of Jesus.

Review

It is important first to review what we have learned about the nature of the Church. Recall the little community of Jesus' followers, gathered in Jerusalem after this passion, death, and resurrection. On Pentecost, The Holy Spirit descends on them, and at once, they go out boldly to preach the Good News about Jesus. The Holy Spirit joins the Church-community to Jesus, so that he, the Risen Lord, is present in the world through his Church. St. Paul calls the Church the "Body of Christ." Think of their physiology. The head is the source of life and activity. It is joined to the body by means of the spirit, and accomplishes what it wants through the body. So too Christ the Head is joined by the Holy Spirit to the Church-community, which is his body. It is Christ who lives and acts through the Church. Therefore, the official actions of the Church are the actions of Christ. We call them the sacraments. In each of the sacraments it is the risen Lord who acts, and whom we meet. We meet him above all in the Holy Eucharist, where he is truly and substantially present to us in his glorified humanity. The Eucharist is at the heart of Catholic life. We will consider the evidence for the Church's teaching on the Eucharist, and then look more closely at the meaning of the Eucharist.

The Promise of the Eucharist

Read *John* 6: 22-69. This is the famous "Bread of Life" chapter in *John*. It begins with an account of the miraculous feeding of five thousand people with five loaves and two fish (1-14). Then it tells of Jesus coming to his disciples, walking on the water, as they make their way across the lake in a boat (15-21).

Now, at verse 22, the crowds who had been fed the day before come looking for Jesus on the other side of the lake. We can understand their search. The feeding was an astonishing sign and they want to see more. Jesus, of course, knows their motivation and challenges them to seek not just earthly food but the food that "endures for eternal life."

At verse 35, Jesus says to them, "I am the bread of life." In the verses that follow, up to verse 47, it is clear that what Jesus means here is that his teaching is "bread" or "food": "Whoever believes in me will never be thirsty." "This is indeed the will of my Father, that all who see the Son and believe in him may have eternal life; and I will raise them up on the last day."

At verse 48, there is a clear change in meaning. There Jesus says again, "I am the bread of life." In verse 51, he says, "I am the living bread that came down from heaven. Whoever eats of this bread will live forever; and the bread that I will give for the life of the world is my flesh." Jesus' hearers immediately spot the change of meaning. They ask, in verse 52: "How can this man give us his flesh to eat." Notice that Jesus does not say: "You misunderstood me," or "You are distorting my words." Instead, he repeats what he said, and emphasizes it to make it abundantly clear: "Very truly I tell you, unless you eat the flesh of the Son of Man and drink his blood you have no life in you. Those who eat my flesh and rink my blood have eternal life, and I will raise them up on the last day; for my flesh is true food and my blood is true drink. Those who eat my flesh and drink my blood abide in me, and I in them. Just as the living Father sent me, and I live because of the Father, so whoever eats me will live because of me. This is the bread that came down from heaven, not like that which your ancestors ate, and they died. But the one who eats this bread will live forever."

In verse 60, we are told, "When many of his disciples heard it, they said: 'This teaching is difficult. Who can accept it'?" At verse 66, we read, "Because of this many of his disciples turned back and no longer went about with him." Again, Jesus does not say, "You misunderstood. Come back!" Rather he turns to the twelve and asks, "Do you also wish to go away?" (verse 67). Simon Peter speaks in the name of all of them and gives the only answer any of us can give: "Lord, to whom can we go? You have the words of eternal life. We have come to believe and know that you are the Holy One of God" (verses 68-9).

The passage is abundantly clear. Jesus is promising that in some way we cannot yet understand, he is going to give us his own flesh to eat and his blood to drink.

The Institution

This takes place at the Last Supper. Look at the scene in *Mark* 14:22-24. (A similar account of the institution of the Eucharist is found in *Matthew* 26: 26-29, and in *Luke* 22: 14-23). Again, note the language. Jesus does not say: "This bread represents my body" or "This is a symbol of my body." He says "This *is* my body" and "This *is* my blood."

Testimony of the Early Church

We may feel that we are misunderstanding the words of the Last Supper. How can this really be Jesus' body and blood? Yet how did the first

Christians understand the words? Here we have some clear testimony. Read *I Corinthians* 11:17-28. This is the earliest written reference to the Eucharist in the New Testament, much earlier than the Gospels, for example. This was written about 54 A.D., some 20 years after the resurrection. Consider the background to this letter, and then look at what it says.

Paul had spent considerable time at Corinth, instructing people and building up the Christian community there. Now he has gone on to Ephesus. There he hears that there are questions that have arisen in the Church at Corinth and some forms of behaviour that need to be corrected. So he writes to answer their questions and to correct their behaviour. One thing that has been reported to him is that they are not acting as they should when they gather for the celebration of the Eucharist. As the letter itself explains, they are making this an occasion for a big meal. Even more, it is also sometimes a meal at which they do not share with one another, or one at which they have too much to drink. He reprimands their conduct by reminding them of what the Eucharist is.

What makes this such a strong testimony to the meaning of the Eucharist is not only Paul's clear statement of what the Eucharist is (and so of how they should conduct themselves when they celebrate it) but his assertion that the teaching he handed on to them is the teaching he himself had received. "Handed on" is the literal meaning of the word "tradition." Paul has given to them the tradition he himself had received. What he says about the Eucharist is the traditional teaching of the Church.

After reading the clear description of the institution of the Eucharist in verses 23 to 26, we notice what Paul concludes in verse 27: "Whoever, therefore, eats the bread or drinks the cup of the Lord in an unworthy manner will be answerable for the body and blood of the Lord." Again, notice the strong language of verse 29: "For all who eat and drink without discerning the body, eat and drink judgment against themselves." (Some ancient manuscripts read "the Lord's body" in verse 29). St. Paul's language here clearly presupposes an understanding of the Eucharist as the actual body and blood of the Lord.

Witness of Early Writers

When we turn to the writings of people in leadership positions in the Church of the first centuries, we again find clear and unambiguous testimony to the belief that the Eucharist is the true body and blood of Jesus Christ. The following are a few of those early testimonies. (The actual texts are given in Appendix I)

(a) St. Justin Martyr, martyred about 165 A.D. in Rome. His description of the Eucharist as celebrated in the early Church is clear. This selection from Justin is read each year in the Prayer of the Church (the "Breviary") on the Third Sunday of Easter.

(b) The Jerusalem Catecheses, about 345 A.D. (This appears in the Breviary on the Saturday within the Octave of Easter).

(c) St. Irenaeus, about 185 A.D. (This account is in the Breviary on Thursday of the 3rd week of Easter).

(d) Tertullian, about 200 A.D. (This account can be found in O'Collins, *op. cit.* p. 259).

The Theological Explanation of the Eucharist

Catholic teaching on the change of the bread and wine into the Body and Blood of Jesus Christ is usually expressed in language taken from the writing of St. Thomas Aquinas. The change is described as "transubstantiation." What this means is that the whole substance of bread and wine is changed into the whole substance of the Body and Blood of Jesus, with only the appearances of bread and wine remaining. The distinction between substance and appearances is that between "what a thing is" and "how it appears" (its accidental features). The appearances of food (shape, taste, size, etc.) remain in the Eucharist, but the reality is now the Body and Blood of Jesus Christ.

Catholic Practice

Since the actual substance of the bread and wine is changed into the substance of Jesus' Body and Blood, it follows that the Lord remains present in the Eucharist as long as the appearances of food remain. For this reason the sacred Hosts that remain after Mass has ended are reserved in the tabernacle.

They are kept safely there so that the Eucharist can be taken to the sick or dying, and so that we can spend time in prayer before the Lord. The sanctuary light that we see in a Catholic Church is a sign that the Blessed Eucharist is present in the tabernacle. This also explains the genuflection that Catholics make when they enter a Catholic Church. It is a sign of our belief that Our Lord Jesus Christ is truly present in the tabernacle; remember that people genuflect only to God. We can see why Catholics place special value on prayer before the Blessed Sacrament, and why we keep the Church open during the day where it is safe to do so.

The Mass

The Mass is dealt with in some detail in the next chapter. For now, we simply emphasize that, because it is truly Jesus present in the Eucharist, the Mass really is Jesus among us, offering his perfect sacrifice, his perfect obedience of the cross, to the Father again, at our hands, and offering us along with Him. The Mass is not something we watch, but something we do.

Why Jesus Comes to us Under the Sign of Food

The sacraments are signs that make present what they signify. They are also meetings with Christ. In the Eucharist, Jesus, by using the sign of food, shows us what he wants to be for us in this meeting. Consider the following example. Suppose you arrange a meeting with a trusted friend because you want to discuss something that is troubling you. At the end of the meeting, you say, "You have been a real comfort to me." It is as if your friend was wearing a sign that read "comfort." So too we can think of Jesus, whom we meet in the Eucharist, as wearing a sign to indicate what he wants to be for us in this meeting. The sign he wears can be thought of as one that reads "food." Consider what food does for us. It gives us strength; it enables us to grow; it even keeps us alive. So too, Jesus, in this meeting with us, wants to strengthen us, to enable us to grow as his disciple and friend, and to be the source of new life for us.

Moreover, since we usually receive the Eucharist together at Mass, he is present as our common banquet or meal. Just as a meal together unites a family, so he wants to be our bond of union, making us a people joined more firmly to him and to one another.

The Eucharist looks back to the manna in the desert. Like the manna, Jesus is our food for the journey. It also looks to the present. We receive the Eucharist together at the same table. By joining us to Christ and to one another, it builds up the Church here and now. Finally, the Eucharist also looks to the future. It is the pledge of future glory, because it is the promise that we will one day be gathered around the Risen Lord in the Kingdom. This imperfect presence of Jesus looks forward to his presence face-to-face with us in our heavenly homeland.

Receiving Communion *NB*

The conditions for receiving the Holy Eucharist, assuming that we are in full communion with the Church, are (a) freedom from serious sin; (b) reflection on what we are doing, and so a reverent and prayerful approach to the Eucharist; (c) faith, and that is why we reply "Amen" to the Eucharistic Minister when we hear the words, "the Body of Christ" and "the Blood of Christ;" (d) fasting from food and drink for at least one hour. All these conditions being supposed, we may receive the Eucharist whenever we are present and taking part in the Mass, even more than once a day. We may also receive under the appearances of either bread or wine or both. It does not matter because Jesus is present as a substance, under the sign of food, in the appearances of both bread and wine.

Video
What Catholics Believe About the Eucharist (Liguori)

Appendix I

EARLY CHRISTIAN WITNESSES TO THE EUCHARIST

St. Justin Martyr (Martyred in Rome about 165 A.D.): *From the First Apology in Defense of the Christians*

"No one may share the eucharist with us unless he believes that what we teach is true, unless he is washed in the regenerating waters of baptism for the remission of his sins, and unless he lives in accordance with the principles given us by Christ.

"We do not consume the eucharistic bread and wine as if it were ordinary food and drink, for we have been taught that as Jesus Christ our Saviour became a man of flesh and blood by the power of the Word of God, so also the food that our flesh and blood assimilates for its nourishment becomes the flesh and blood of the incarnate Jesus by the power of his own words contained in the prayer of thanksgiving.

"The apostles, in their recollections, which are called gospels, handed down to us what Jesus commanded them to do. They tell us that he took bread, gave thanks, and said, 'Do this in memory of me. This is my body.' In the same way he took the cup, he gave thanks and said, 'This is my blood.' The Lord gave this command to them alone. Ever since then we have constantly reminded one another of these things. The rich among us help the poor and we are always united. For all that we receive we praise the Creator of the universe through his Son Jesus Christ and through the Holy Spirit.

"On Sunday we have a common assembly of all our members, whether they live in the city or in the outlying districts. The recollections of the apostles or the writings of the prophets are read, as long as there is time. When the reader has finished, the president of the assembly speaks to us; he urges everyone to imitate the examples of virtue we have heard in the readings. Then we all stand up together and pray.

"At the conclusion of our prayer, bread and wine and water are brought forward. The president offers prayers and gives thanks to the best of his ability, and the people give their assent by saying 'Amen'. The eucharist is distributed, everyone present communicates, and the deacons take it to those who are absent.

"The wealthy, if they wish, may make a contribution, and they themselves decide the amount. The collection is placed in the custody of the president, who uses it to help the orphans and widows and all who for any reason are in distress, whether because they are sick, in prison, or away from home. In a word, he takes care of all who are in need.

"We hold our common assembly on Sunday because it is the first day of the week, the day on which God put darkness and chaos to flight and created the world, and because on that same day our Saviour Jesus Christ rose from the dead. For he was crucified on Friday and on Sunday he appeared to his apostles and disciples and taught them the things that we have passed on for your consideration."

St. Cyril of Jerusalem (about 345 A.D.): The Jerusalem Catecheses

" 'On the night he was betrayed our Lord Jesus Christ took bread, and when he had given thanks, he broke it and gave it to his disciples and said: Take, eat: this is my body. He took the cup, gave thanks, and said, Take, drink: this is my blood.' Since Christ himself has declared the bread to be his body, who can have any further doubt? Since he himself has said quite categorically, 'This is my blood', who would dare to question it and say that it was not his blood?

"Therefore it is with complete assurance that we receive the bread and wine as the body and blood of Christ. His body is given to us under the symbol of bread, and his blood is given to us under the symbol of wine, in order to make us by receiving them one body and blood with him. Having his body and blood in our members, we become bearers of Christ and sharers, as Saint Peter says, in the divine nature.

"Once, when speaking to the Jews, Christ said: 'Unless you eat my flesh and drink my blood you shall have no life in you.' This horrified them and they left him. Not understanding his words in a spiritual way, they thought the Saviour wished them to practice cannibalism.

"Under the old covenant there was showbread, but it came to an end with the old dispensation to which it belonged. Under the new covenant, there is bread from heaven and the cup of salvation. These sanctify both soul and body, the bread being adapted to the sanctification of the body, the Word, to the sanctification of the soul.

"We do not, then, regard the Eucharistic elements as ordinary bread and wine: they are in fact the body and blood of the Lord, as he himself has declared. Whatever your senses may tell you, be strong in faith."

St. Irenaeus (about 185 A.D.) Treatise Against Heresies

"If our flesh is not saved, then the Lord has not redeemed us with his blood, the Eucharistic chalice does not make us sharers in his blood, and the bread we break does not make us sharers in his body. There can be no blood without veins, flesh, and the rest of the human substance, and this the Word of God actually became; it was with his own blood that he redeemed us. As the Apostle says, 'In him, through his blood, we have been redeemed, our sins have been forgiven.'

"We are his members and we are nourished by creation, which is his gift to us, for it is he who causes the sun to rise and the rain to fall. He declared that the chalice, which comes from his creation, was his blood; and he makes it the nourishment of our blood. He affirmed that the bread, which comes from his creation, was his body, and he makes it the nourishment of our body. When the chalice we mix and the bread we bake receive the word of God, the Eucharistic elements become the body and blood of Christ, by which our bodies live and grow. How then can it be said that the flesh belonging to the Lord's own body and nourished by his body and blood is incapable of receiving God's gift of eternal life? Saint Paul says in his letter to the Ephesians that 'we are members of his body', of his flesh and bones. He is not speaking of some spiritual and incorporeal kind of man, 'for spirits do not have flesh and bones.' He is speaking of a real human body composed of flesh, sinews, and bones, nourished by the chalice of Christ's blood and receiving growth from the bread which is his body.

"The slip of a vine planted in the ground bears fruit at the proper time. The grain of wheat falls into the ground and decays only to be raised up again and multiplied by the Spirit of God who sustains all things. The Wisdom of God places these things at the service of man and when they receive God's word, they become the eucharist, which is the body and blood of Christ. In the same way, our bodies, which have been nourished by the eucharist, will be buried in the earth and will decay, but they will rise again at the appointed time, for the Word of God will raise them up to the glory of God the Father. Then the Father will clothe our mortal nature in immortality and freely endow our corruptible nature with incorruptibility, for God's power is shown most perfectly in weakness."

Tertullian (about 200 A.D.) De Resurrectione Carnis

"No soul whatever is able to obtain salvation unless it has believed while it was in the flesh. Indeed, the flesh is the very condition on which salvation hinges …. The flesh is washed [baptism], so that the soul may be cleansed. The flesh is anointed, so that the soul may be consecrated. The flesh is signed [with the cross], so that the soul too may be fortified. The flesh is overshadowed by the imposition of hands [confirmation], so that the soul may be illuminated by the Spirit. The flesh feeds on the body and blood of Christ [the Eucharist], so that the soul likewise may feed on its God. They [the body and soul] cannot then be separated in their reward, when they are united in their service."

Appendix II

THE EUCHARIST AND THE REFORMATION

1500 Years of Tradition

"Nothing is more solid than the unanimity of belief in the Real Presence of Christ in the Eucharist for the first 1500 years of the Church. The spontaneous uproar caused by men such as Berengarius of Tours (d. 1088) only attests the more to the unquestioned acceptance of the Real Presence. This unanimous belief of 1,500 years is itself an argument to its truth. For it is impossible that the Holy Spirit, the Spirit of Truth, could leave the Church in error over a long period of time about one of the central doctrines of Christianity." (*The New Catholic Encyclopedia*, Vol. 5, p.604)

Positions of Reformers on the Eucharist

Luther – did not totally deny the Real Presence of Christ in the Eucharist. He was quite firm on this. What he proposed was a doctrine of "consubstantiation" according to which the Body and Blood of Christ become truly present in the Eucharist *along with* the bread and wine. However, he also said that Christ was present only at the moment of receiving Communion and was not present in the Hosts that remain after Mass.

Zwingli – believed that Luther was not being true to his own principles here. He went beyond Luther and held that Christ is present in the Eucharist only *symbolically*. So communion with Christ in the Eucharist is achieved only through the faith of the recipient.

Calvin – took a middle position. He said that Christ is present in the Eucharist not only symbolically but also by his special *power* that flows from the Body of Christ in heaven into the souls of those who receive the Sacrament. This is referred to as a "dynamic presence," as opposed to the purely "symbolic" presence of Zwingli and the "realistic" presence of Luther.

Causes of Reformers' Views on the Eucharist

First, the Reformation principle of justification by faith alone. Luther's personal experience is an important factor. As a young man, he was tormented by the thought of damnation. Influenced by the views of Ockham (which were somewhat Pelagian), he felt that his salvation depended on what he himself did, and he seemed unable to do anything to overcome sin in himself. Nothing brought him peace. Then his reading of the Epistle to the Romans brought him to the conviction that one is justified simply by faith in the Gospel. Justification is not an internal change in the sinner but simply a declaration by Christ that God covers over one's faults. Humans themselves however remain totally corrupt. Hence, nothing the human person does can be of any benefit. All human works, including reception of the Sacraments, are of no avail to salvation. Hence, there is no place for sacraments in the traditional or Catholic sense.

Second, Luther was appalled by the abuses he saw around him of priests seeking payment for the saying of Mass and of people having an almost magical view of what the sacraments could do for them. In this respect, he wanted to be a true reformer of the Church. A Catholic would argue that his reforming zeal took him too far.

Third, the influence of Berengarius is a factor. In the 9th century, there had been a controversy between two Benedictines, Radbertus and Ratramnus, concerning the correct interpretation of St. Augustine's teaching on the Eucharist in the 4th century. St. Augustine speaks of the sign value of the sacraments, and Ratrumnus misunderstood this to mean that the sacraments are *only* signs. Hence the Eucharist is only a symbol of the Body and Blood of Christ. In the 11th century, Berengarius, influenced by the writing of Ratrumnus, denied the real presence of Christ in the Eucharist (though he later changed his position). This position was later adopted by John Wyclif in England, and then by Zwingli and Karlstadt on the Continent.

Chapter 6

 **THE MASS**

"It now seems clear that the Reformation was indeed achieved in England against the tide of popular conviction. The English people in the early sixteenth century were overwhelmingly Catholic, and the early Tudor Church was, by and large, popular and effective. . . What is abundantly clear, however, is that the majority of the Tudor laity were anything but alienated from the Catholic Church. They understood, valued, and enthusiastically participated in the religion it offered them. And it is now increasingly clear that for the most part they abandoned that religion with extreme reluctance." (Eamon Duffy, *"The Reformation Revisited," The Tablet*, March 4, 1995, p. 280. Duffy teaches Church History at Cambridge University).

English Catholics were very devoted to the Mass, and they deeply resented having it taken away from them. In a couple of Duffy's book-length studies, records show that people hid the vestments and missals so they would not be destroyed. Later on, of course, priests offered Mass in secret, and a number of them, such as St. Edmund Campion, were put to death for doing so. In Ireland, when Britain imposed penal laws there, the Irish became resourceful in finding ways for priests to offer Mass in secret. The Mass is not an incidental to Catholicism; it is at the heart of Catholic life and practice. What is the Mass?

The Mass is a Sacrifice

On the *cross*, Jesus offered himself for us. His perfect obedience to the Father, even to death on the cross, was offered in our name, and on our behalf. "No one has greater love than this, to lay down one's life for one's friends." (*John* 15:13).

In turn, Jesus' words at the *Last Supper* make it clear that he was offering there the same sacrifice that would take place next day on the cross. This can be seen from his words at the Last Supper: "This is my body *which is given for you*" (*Luke* 22:19); "This is my blood of the covenant *which is poured out for many for the forgiveness of sins*" (*Matthew* 26:28).

The Sacrifice of the Mass is to be Offered by the Church

Jesus has given this sacrifice *to his Church*, so that in the Mass this one sacrifice is offered again and again. Note that in the Last Supper accounts in the New Testament, Jesus told his disciples, "Do this in memory of me." He *ordered* his followers to do what he had done at the Last Supper.

"*In memory of me:*" Consider what "memory" meant for the Jews in this context. Every time the Jews celebrated (remembered) the Passover, they believed the Exodus events were made present to them so that they might conform their lives to them. However, in the New Testament, "memorial" means far more. When the Church celebrates the Eucharist, the sacrifice Christ offered on the cross once for all is made present in a much fuller way, by the bread and wine being changed into Jesus' body and blood. The Eucharist re-presents (makes present) the sacrifice of the cross and applies its fruit to us.

The Mass is the *sacrament* of the sacrifice Jesus offered on the cross. Keep in mind what is meant by a "sacrament." It is a sign that makes present that of which it is the sign. In the Mass, Jesus' offering of himself on the cross is made present to us sacramentally. At Mass Jesus offers his sacrifice at our hands, in our name, on our behalf.

The sacrifice of the *Cross* and the sacrifice of the *Eucharist* are one single sacrifice. The victim and the priest are the same; the same victim who offered himself on the cross now offers himself through the action of the Church's ministerial priests. Only the manner of offering is different, bloody on the Cross, unbloody in the Mass. Christ is the principal agent of the Mass; it is he who presides invisibly over every Eucharist.

The Mass was an essential element in the life of the *first Christians*. "They devoted themselves to the apostles' teaching and fellowship, to the breaking of bread and the prayers" (*Acts* 2:42. Cf. 2:46). ("The breaking of bread" was the early name for the Eucharist.) They did this especially on Sunday, the day of the Lord's resurrection: "On the first day of the week, when we met to break bread, Paul was holding a discussion with them" (*Acts* 20:7). This is also the early witness of Justin Martyr (writing about 155 A.D.). We saw his words in our discussion on the Eucharist. They can also be read in *The Catechism of the Catholic Church*, no. 1345.

The Whole Church is Offered in the Mass

When the Church offers the sacrifice of Christ, she offers herself along with him. The lives of the faithful, with all their works, prayers, etc. are offered along with Christ, and this total offering gives them a new value.

Therefore, when we are at Mass, we are *not just spectators*. All of us are offering the sacrifice of Christ along with the ministerial priest, and we are offering ourselves along with Christ.

Those in heaven offer themselves along with us also.

Consider the following important statements about the Mass:
- It is the perfect sacrifice of *praise* and thanksgiving to the Father
- It is a sign of *unity* that joins us to Christ and to one another, and so builds up the Church.
- It is the great *banquet* in which we receive Christ the Lord, and so is also a foreshadowing and pledge of the future heavenly banquet. The Altar of Sacrifice is also the Table of the Lord
- The Mass, therefore, is the *supreme prayer*. We need to realize what is happening at Mass. It is something far beyond any *private prayer* we could offer, or could offer at home. So people who deliberately absent themselves from Mass, and say: "I pray at home," or "I pray in my heart," or "I pray in the woods," lack a genuine awareness of what the Mass is.

The Parts of the Mass

The Mass is divided into two parts: The Liturgy of the Word, and the Liturgy of the Eucharist. This is reflected in the sanctuary where we find both the pulpit with the Scriptures, and the Altar. Note the difference here from most Protestant Churches, which see Christ present only, or primarily, in the Word of God, and so whose sanctuaries usually feature only a pulpit with the Scriptures.

In a later chapter, we will see something about the Liturgical Year. We will also say something then about the three-year cycle of Readings for the

Mass.

For a more *detailed* explanation of the Mass, see the Appendix.

Video

Understanding the Liturgy of the Mass (Liguori)

Appendix

THE MASS

The Name
- "The breaking of the bread" (*Acts of The Apostles* and *I Corinthians*)
- "The Lord's Supper" (*I Corinthians*)
- "The Eucharist" (Post-apostolic times). Means "Thanksgiving"
- "Sacrifice" (2nd and 3rd century)
- "The Liturgy" (Early times in Rome, but then mostly in the East). Means "Public Worship"
- *Synaxis* and *Collecta*. Means "Gathering"
- *Missa* or "Mass" – came to be common name in West. At end of Latin Mass, priest said, "*Ite Missa Est*" ("Go, it is the sending or mission"). The congregation was thereby dismissed and sent out to *live* the Mass.

Why did "The Mass" come to be the common name? Well, the priest dismissed the people with a *blessing* at the end of Mass when he said "*Ite Missa Est*" (as indeed he still does). So "missa" came to be associated with the notion of "a blessing." Moreover the entire Mass came to be regarded as a "blessing" because during it the bread and wine are "blessed" or consecrated and so changed into the Body and Blood of Christ.

The Two Main Parts of the Mass
The Mass is divided into the Liturgy of the Word and the Liturgy of the Eucharist. These are not just two parts added together. Rather the Liturgy of the Word is ordered to the Liturgy of the Eucharist. The one part prepares for the other.

By hearing God's Word, the Church grows in wisdom. By participating in the Eucharist, the Church grows in holiness. The Word and the Eucharist both nourish the Church.

The Liturgy of the Word
This liturgy is adapted from the Jewish Sabbath Synagogue Service.

Originally, Jewish Christians continued to attend the Synagogue. Afterwards they would gather at one of their homes for the Eucharist. After Jewish Christians were expelled from the Synagogue (about 44 A.D.), they got into the practice of having a Liturgy of the Word prior to their celebration of the Eucharist. [It is helpful here to recall the evolution the early Christian community went through as it gradually realized that Gentiles did not need to become Jews first in order to become Christians. Then of course, Christians, separated from the Synagogue, began to observe the Sabbath on Sundays, partly because this was the day Jesus rose from the dead, and partly to distinguish themselves from other Jews.]

To understand the liturgy of the Word, we need to realize that Christ is truly *present* to us in his Word. It is an active, living Word. Christ is the centre of the Scriptures: hidden in the Old Testament, fully brought to light in the New Testament.

The Mass really begins with what used to be called the *Introit.* In practice today, this is the processional hymn. So that hymn is really part of the Mass. It is important to be there for it!

The first thing we have after the Processional Hymn is the *Kyrie* and the *Collect* (Opening Prayer). These originally belonged together, and the *Gloria* was only inserted between them afterwards (as we will see below).

The idea is that we come to Mass as petitioners or beggars. At the start of Mass the congregation first brought before God its petitions or needs and concerns. Each was presented, perhaps by the Deacon, and the response was "Kyrie Eleison," that is "Lord have mercy." This could be lengthy. Then at the end, all of these petitions were "summed up" or "collected" in the *Collect,* that is, the opening Prayer.

The *"Kyrie"* – As it stands today, all nine of these petitions are addressed to Jesus. The Kyrie in its present form was moved to the start of the Mass in the 4th or 5th century. There are many musical forms of the Kyrie.

The *"Gloria"* – This Trinitarian hymn was inserted here in the Mass in the 6th century. Note the specifically Christian character of what we are praising in this hymn. At first it was only recited by the Bishop (the "Angel" or Shepherd of the Church), and even then only on special occasions. It began to appear in most Masses, even those just celebrated by the priest, in the 11th century. The Gloria is one of the most ancient examples of hymns in the early Church. It was highly esteemed, even though it is not taken from the Bible. It has its origin in early Syrian and Greek Christian communities. The Latin text of it dates from the 7th century. It is called the "Greater Doxology" (as distinguished from the "Glory be to the Father, etc."). It was also known as the "Hymn of the Angels." There are many different melodies for the Gloria.

The *Readings* – These are not just a matter of antiquarian interest. Rather it is Christ himself who speaks to us when these readings are proclaimed, in the Mass and in the Sacramental liturgies.

The *Responsorial Psalm* – This is a meditative response to the first reading.

The *Homily* – Applies the readings to our lives, and especially is meant to dispose us so that we can participate well in this Eucharist. While the priest has a great responsibility to prepare this well, the congregation has a corresponding responsibility to listen attentively, to the readings and to the homily.

The *Creed* – This was not originally in the Mass, and was not added until 1014. It is really part of the Baptismal liturgy. Today it serves as our response to the Word of God, an expression of our faith in what we have heard.

The *General Intercessions* – These now conclude the Liturgy of the Word.

The Liturgy of the Eucharist

The Eucharist is the Banquet. So the Offertory is the setting of the table; the Preface-Eucharistic Prayer is the table-blessing; the Communion is the eating.

The *Offertory* – prepares the matter that is to be offered in the Sacrifice. At the same time, it aims to instill in us sentiments of self-offering, so that we offer ourselves along with the Victim.

The *Washing of the Hands* – This action symbolizes internal purification. At one time, it was physically necessary because the priest had handled the various gifts brought forward.

The *Preface-Canon* – is one continuous prayer, an act of thanksgiving for

God's redemptive action, reaching its climax in the *renewal* of that action in the narrative of the Institution of the Eucharist.

The *Sanctus (Holy, Holy, Holy)* – is a part of this prayer of thanksgiving. It gives the people a part in the Consecratory Prayer.

The *Elevation of the Host and Chalice* – This began to be practised throughout the Roman Rite only around the 13th century. It was begun for two reasons. *First*, because of the infrequent reception of the Eucharist, people satisfied their devotion just by gazing at the Sacred Host and Precious blood. *Second*, as an antidote to the heresy of Berengarius. In this sense, the practice really began in Gaul, and was meant to give the people an opportunity to make an explicit act of faith in the Real Presence.

After the Consecration, we have the prayers of Offering of the Victim, the Anamnesis. And then we have prayers that express our offering of ourselves along with the Victim.

Conclusion of Eucharistic Prayer – Jesus offer himself to the Father in the Holy Spirit. He also brings all creation, humans included, into this supreme act of glorification of the Father. As he does this, the assembly adds its wholehearted Amen.

The Our Father – begins the Communion rite. In it we ask for our "daily bread," which in a special way refers to the Eucharist. The Our Father was added here by Pope Gregory the Great (6th century).

The Breaking of the Host – Originally, leavened bread was used for the Mass. At this point it had to be broken for the people to receive from it. This took some time. So people sang the *Lamb of God* while this was taking place. It was a much longer song during those centuries than it is today. The Church changed to unleavened bread in the 9-11th centuries.

The Placing of a Particle in the Chalice – This was the "fermentum" – a particle of the Sacred Host sent by the Pope to the Pastors of the Roman churches who could not be present at the Papal Mass. It was meant to be a sign of unity between the Chief Shepherd and the Pastors.

The Sign of Peace – Though it now appears here, it used to be given just before the Offertory.

The Communion – In the beginning all people received under both species, receiving the Sacred Host in their hand, and then receiving from the Chalice. In the 9th century, the practice began of placing Sacred Host on the communicant's tongue. In the11[th] century, the practice of all receiving from the Chalice was discontinued. After Vatican II the practice of receiving also from the Chalice was restored. This is today the recommended practice.

Conclusion of the Mass – With the Prayer after Communion and the final blessing, the Mass ends quite quickly. At the end of Mass in the Roman Rite, the priest used to read the beginning of the Gospel of John. This had begun as a private devotion of the celebrant on his way from the altar. It was discontinued when the Mass was revised after Vatican II.

Chapter 7

THE SACRAMENT OF RECONCILIATION

The New Testament Background to This Sacrament

One of the best-loved parables of Jesus is the story of the Prodigal Son, or, more accurately, the Parable of the Two Sons (*Luke* 15: 11-32). There could be no better introduction to the Sacrament of Reconciliation. It is important at this point to take up this parable and read it carefully.

Jesus used this moving story to show us that God is our Father, who loves us passionately, and who is always there waiting to receive us if only we will acknowledge our sins and turn humbly to him. What this parable illustrates so vividly is that one of the greatest features of the life of Jesus was his reaching out to sinners. He was even criticized for sharing table fellowship with sinners, but his response was, "Those who are well have no need of a physician, but those who are sick. I have come to call not the righteous but sinners." (*Mark* 2:17)

Moreover, Jesus himself actually forgave sins. Only God can forgive sins, as his critics pointed out. Since he is God the Son, Jesus is able to say of himself, "The Son of Man has authority on earth to forgive sins" (cf. *Mark* 2:1-12). Thus, we see him exercising this power on several occasions in his public ministry. For example, to the sinful woman he said, "Your sins are forgiven" (*Luke* 7:47-50).

Since the forgiveness of sinners was so central a feature of Jesus' public life, we would expect that this mercy and forgiveness would be evident still in Jesus' presence among us in his Church. Surely, the Risen Christ, living among us in the Church-community, will continue to be the Divine Physician present to heal us.

We find that is the case. See *John* 20:19-23, where Jesus says, "Receive the Holy Spirit. If you forgive the sins of any, they are forgiven them; if you retain the sins of any, they are retained." Jesus here imparts to his Church his own power to forgive sins. Moreover, this power is to be exercised in an official way by those who share his authority in the Church. Cf. *Matthew* 16:13-19; 18:18: "Whatever you bind on earth will be bound in heaven, and whatever you loose on earth will be loosed in heaven." This power is reflected also in *Matthew* 9:1-8: "When the crowds saw it they were filled with awe, and they glorified God who had given such authority to human beings." The plural form used here, "human beings," is generally considered to reflect the situation in Matthew's Church where people did receive forgiveness of their sins from their human leaders.

The Exercise of this Sacrament in the Early Church

We do see the early Church exercising this power of forgiveness of sins. One of the early Christian writers, Tertullian, spoke of it as "the second plank [of salvation] after the shipwreck of sin." The first plank, of course, was Baptism. In the early Church people who converted to Christianity and received Baptism were expected not to fall away by committing "death-dealing" sins, such as apostasy, murder, adultery (vs. "daily sins"). Such people *could* be reconciled to the Church again, but only after a long period of penance (often years!), only once in a lifetime, and then in a public reconciliation carried out by the Bishop. Some people like Tertullian and Origen were very rigorous, though the *Didiscalia Apostolorum* in the early 3rd century was more compassionate.

The Council of Nicaea (325) insisted that the Church had the authority to reconcile sinners, even those who had lapsed during persecution, but it preserved the rigorous conditions mentioned above.

By the late 4th or early 5th century the administration of reconciliation was entrusted in some places also to priests and it began to involve the obligation of secrecy on the part of the priest.

Beginning about the end of the 6th century there was a dramatic change. Irish and Anglo-Saxon monk-missionaries began the tradition in Europe (which they re-evangelized after the Barbarian invasions) of private confession, and regular, even frequent, reception of the sacrament, even for venial sins, to help people make progress in the Christian life. They also ended the "once-in-a-lifetime" rule for grave sins, though they imposed severe penances in these cases. (The distinction between "mortal" or death-dealing sins, that destroy one's friendship with God, and venial sins, that weaken but do not destroy it, will be considered again in a later chapter).

Present Form of This Sacrament

The form of this sacrament as we know it today is the result of decisions by the 4th Lateran Council (1215), the Council of Florence (1439), the Council of Trent (1551), and the Second Vatican Council (1964). The teaching of the Second Vatican Council on this sacrament is embodied in the new form for the celebration of this sacrament that was promulgated in 1973. This provides for a more inviting setting in a confessional room (as opposed to the old-style "confessional box"). It also includes provision for communal celebrations of this sacrament that combine a shared preparation for the sacrament with individual confession and absolution from one of several confessors taking part. Vatican II sought to restore a sense of the social consequences of our sins, and especially the harm we do to the entire Church-community. That is why reconciliation is not just a matter between God and the individual person; there must also be reconciliation to the Church. In fact, as we shall see, reconciliation with the Church actually is reconciliation with Christ.

There are three acts to this sacrament: confession, contrition, and satisfaction. The confession of sins can be done anonymously (behind a screen) or face-to-face. The most important act is, obviously, contrition. Without genuine contrition on the part of the penitent (as well as an honest confession according to our best ability), the priest's absolution does us no good. Of course, it is also the case that true contrition involves an honest commitment to avoid the occasions of sin and to break our sinful habits.

Frequent confession is encouraged by the Church. Pope Pius XII pointed out the following benefits to this practice: (1) It increases self-knowledge; (2) It promotes growth in humility; (3) It helps overcome bad habits; (4) It overcomes lukewarmness; (5) It strengthens our will and increases self-control; (6) It causes God's grace to grow in us. Clearly, it is also a good occasion for spiritual direction.

This is a good place to say something about the seal of confession. The Church protects this seal (or secrecy) with the most severe penalties. According to Canon 1388, a priest who knowingly and deliberately reveals the identity of the sin and the sinner incurs an automatic excommunication. He can only be absolved by a priest or bishop who has received a mandate from the Apostolic See, that is, the Vatican, to do so, and the penance imposed on him would be severe. Law courts in our country usually respect the secrecy of the confessional. Even if a particular court were to insist that a priest reveal what he knew from confession, he would have to refuse. He would likely then be found in contempt of court and would have to suffer the consequences; every priest knows, however, that this is the decision he would be bound in conscience to make.

Yet Why Confess our Sins to a Priest?

Protestants often object at this point that they do indeed believe in the need to confess our sins, to stir up sorrow for them, and to seek God's forgiveness. Yet they protest that they go directly to God in order to do this. Why do they need to confess to a priest? Why put someone between myself and God? There are two important responses to this objection.

First, it reflects an inadequate understanding of the *Church*. To be a Christian is not just to be an individual relating in an invisible way to God. To be a Christian is to be part of the Church-community. Here is the key consideration: Christ is present to us in this community. It is here in the Church-community that we find Christ. That is the meaning of Pentecost. Here Jesus is truly present, to forgive us, heal us, teach us, strengthen us. So, we do go directly to God for forgiveness, but this is where we find God in a privileged way. Jesus, the Risen Lord, lives, and acts in the world through his Church-community. The Church is not something between Jesus and me; it is the special presence of Jesus to me.

Second, it reflects an inadequate understanding of *sin*. Most of us tend to think of sin as a purely individual matter, something simply between God and me. Of course, it is far more than that. Sin is a social reality. My sins have all sorts of consequences for others, even sins that I commit in private, because they make me into a certain kind of person, and that is reflected in my dealing with others. In particular, when I sin, I fail the other members of the Church-community. I let them down, and I compromise the sign that the entire Church is called to be in our world. I go over to the enemy. So my sins don't just offend God; they also fail my brothers and sisters in the Church-community. That is why I have to be reconciled with the Church-community. I do this through the official representative of that community, that is, the priest.

Reconciliation with the Church is actually reconciliation with Christ. The Church is the presence of Christ. What we do to the Church we do to Christ. "Saul, Saul, why do you persecute me?" (*Acts of the Apostles* 9:4), Jesus asked of Saul when he appeared to him on the road to Damascus. Of course, it was the Church that Saul had been persecuting. Therefore, when the priest reconciles us with the Church, that very act reconciles us with Christ. The one act is the sacrament of the other.

Method of Confessing

A good preparation is essential. (a) An examination of conscience to see what sins or sinful practices have been part of our life since our last confession. The best way to prepare for this is to make a good examination of conscience at the end of each day. (b) Even more important is a reflection on the reasons why I should be sorry for my sins: the loss of heaven and the pains of hell, but most of all the offense offered to the all-holy God who is my only true good, my saviour, my lover. (c) Reflection on the steps I intend to take with God's help in order to change my life.

As we prepare for confession, it is good to look behind sins like "being impatient" or "being uncharitable," and ask, "Why am I acting this way?" This gets at the deeper causes of many of our sins, and often points to one of the capital sins (like pride or envy). This is the wise suggestion of St. Francis de Sales.

Here are a couple of suggestions that can help us make a better confession. First, at the start of our confession, mention a line from scripture that has struck us recently and link our confession to that. (This is recommended in the 1974 directive from Rome). Second, it is helpful, before confessing our sins, to mention a few blessings we have received recently. Such blessings might include our health, having a job, etc. When a person does this first, then confesses their sins, and then says, "I am sorry for my sins because God has been so good to me," the person arrives at perfect contrition out of a motive of gratitude. Many people have found this most helpful in making a better confession.

A humble and honest approach to confessing is great medicine for us. It is also helpful to remember that the priest to whom we confess is a sinner too, a fellow Christian who himself goes to confession regularly, and who has heard probably thousands of confessions before hearing ours.

For expressing our sorrow when we go to confession, it is good to know an act of contrition by heart, though we can use any appropriate words of our own, so long as we sincerely mean them.

The priest will assign us a penance – a symbolic action or prayer by which we express our intention to amend our life. We should be careful to fulfill our penance because it is an integral part of the sacrament.

How often should one go to confession? The important thing is to go on a regular basis. This might mean going once a month, or at the start of each new season, or perhaps at what are, for a particular person, key points in the year. Certainly if one is guilty of mortal sin, that person should go to confession as soon as possible.

Video
What Catholics Believe about Reconciliation (Liguori)

Appendix

GOING TO CONFESSION

1. I say to the priest, *Bless me Father, for I have sinned.*
2. After the priest says the prayer of blessing, I say, *It is ... since my last confession.* (I say how long it is since I last confessed)
3. Prior to confessing, I might want to mention a line from scripture that has recently struck me, and link my confession to that. I might also want to mention first some of the blessings in my life, as suggested above, and point to these as a motive for sorrow in having offended the God who has been so good to me.
4. I say, *These are my sins.* Then I tell my sins to the priest. I should speak plainly and briefly, but also try to focus on the underlying causes of my sins.
5. At the end, I say, *I am sorry for these and for all the sins of my life.*
6. I listen carefully to what advice or words of encouragement the priest has for me, and what penance he is assigning to me.
7. When the priest tells me to express sorrow for my sins, I make an act of contrition. (There is an example on the next page).
8. After I complete my act of contrition, the priest says the prayers of forgiveness. At the end of the prayers, I say: *Amen.*
9. When the priest dismisses me, by saying something like *God bless you,* I say, *Thank you, Father*, and I leave.
10. After my confession, if my penance is some prayers I have to say, I say them right away, as carefully as I can. Then I thank God for forgiving my sins. Finally I talk to God about what I intend to do, with God's help, in order to be a better follower of Christ. I should try to have some really practical plan in mind.

PREPARING FOR CONFESSION

1. Examine my conscience, to know better in what ways I have failed God and others since my last confession. Also, try to determine what deeper traits of character and what occasions of sin have led to my faults.
2. Make sure I am truly sorry for having offended God. It helps to look at a crucifix, to see there how greatly Jesus has loved me. It also helps to remember that the only really important thing in life is to live in such a way that I will reach eternal life with God.
3. Decide what things I can do to become a better person, a better follower of Jesus.

AN ACT OF CONTRITION

O my God I am truly sorry for having offended you, and I detest my sins, not only because by them I have lost all right to heaven and have deserved the everlasting suffering of hell, but especially because they offend you, my God, who are so good and deserving of all my love. I firmly resolve, with the help of your grace, to sin no more, and to avoid the occasions that lead to sin. Amen.

AN ADULT EXAMINATION OF CONSCIENCE

1. Have I spent time in prayer every day?
    Is God real in my life, someone with whom I feel comfortable?
    Do I really put God ahead of everything else in my life?
2. Have I used the Name of God without respect?
    Have I misused the great gift of speech in other ways with improper language?
3. Have I missed Mass on Sundays through my own fault?
    Do I make a sincere effort to participate in Mass?
4. Have I failed in my duty of respect and love to my parents? To my children?
    Have I seriously broken the laws of the land, such as traffic laws?
    Am I honestly able to say that I love my neighbour as myself?
    Am I respectful of others? Of the poor? Of people who are different from

me, or who disagree with me?

5. Have I been unkind to others? Have I harmed others in any way?
   Have I subjected others to my bad temper?
   Have I eaten, drunk or used anything in a way that could hurt my health, or that shows lack of respect for my own person?

6. Have I been guilty of sins against chastity, alone or with others?
   If I am married, have I been unfaithful to my spouse in any way? Have I sinned against marriage in other ways, such as by not being open to new life?
   Have I treated others in a way that fails to respect their privacy and dignity?
   Have I done anything that makes me more self-centered and less loving to others?

7. Have I stolen anything? Have I damaged the property of others?
   Have I been honest in my business dealings, in my payment of my employees, in my work, in my shopping?
   Have I been generous with what I have, and been ready to share with the needy?
   Have I treated others in a way that is not fair to them?

8. Have I been untruthful?
   Have I gossiped about others, or talked in a way that unnecessarily harmed others?
   Have I talked too much about myself and not listened to others?
   Have I violated the confidence of others?

9. Have I deliberately thought about impure actions?
   Have I watched things on television, the movies, or the internet, that incline me to sin or to treat others selfishly?

10. Have I been envious of others, or jealous of the success of others?
    Have I indulged in unnecessary or extravagant purchases?
    Have I failed to be grateful to God or to others?

Chapter 8

THE SACRAMENT OF MATRIMONY

Of the seven sacraments, two are *social sacraments*: Matrimony and Holy Orders. In other words, these two sacraments strengthen the person, not just for that person's own benefit, but also for the good of the whole Church-community. Married couples carry out important social roles, and this sacrament equips them to do that. In this sense, Matrimony and Holy Orders are similar to one another.

What is Marriage?

Canon 1055: "The matrimonial covenant, by which a man and a woman establish between themselves a partnership of the whole of life, is by its nature ordered toward the good of the spouses and the procreation and education of offspring; this covenant between baptized persons has been raised by Christ the Lord to the dignity of a sacrament."

Let us examine that further.

First, marriage is not just a human plan but is God's plan. Cf. *Genesis* 2:18-24. This passage of Sacred Scripture makes it clear that this covenant between a man and a woman was God's plan right from the beginning. That is why it is so deeply rooted in us. As the text makes clear, the union between husband and wife is greater even than that between parent and child. "Leave father and mother," the spouses are told.

Since marriage is God's plan, this means that it is also a wise plan; it works; it perfects the parties who enter into it. Marriage illustrates the truth that we are truly capable of making commitments for life, and that such commitments are creative, they make us grow as persons.

Second, marriage is a public contract, not just a private one. That is one of the reasons why the law (both Church law and civil law) requires that there be witnesses to it. Society has a stake in it, for many reasons. (a) The faithfulness involved in marriage is a source of social stability. (b) The care and education of children in marriage is very much a social concern. It has been established that one of the greatest sources of poverty among children is the breakdown of marriage. (c) The great social virtues, such as civility, hospitality, generosity, solidarity, and dialogue are learned within a stable family.

This public feature of marriage needs great emphasis today, because in our individualistic society this great social union of marriage is more and more being looked upon by people as "a personal arrangement," a "personal preference," and therefore as just "one lifestyle option among others."

Third, marriage is something total, not just something partial. The intimate physical gift that two people make of themselves to one another in marriage is the outward sign and symbol of the gift they make of their lives to one another. This is one of the things we mean when we call marriage a covenant, based on God's love for his people in the Old Testament and Christ's love for his Church in the New Testament, rather than just a "contract."

Fourth, marriage between baptized persons is a sacrament. See *John* 2:1-11: the presence and actions of Jesus at the wedding-feast at Cana already indicate that Jesus raised the covenant of marriage to a sacrament. (John calls Jesus' change of water into wine at Cana the first of his signs. It is a "sign" that Jesus has come to make all things new, including human institutions, like marriage.) *Ephesians* 5:21-33 makes this sacramental reality explicit.

When two baptized persons enter into a valid marriage, then, it is also a sacrament, which they, as baptized Christians, confer on one another. The mutual consent of the couples, exchanged in the presence of the priest and two witnesses, actually constitutes the sacrament in the Latin Rite. This sacrament: (a) makes this couple a sign to the world of God's love and faithfulness; and (b) gives this couple a title to the graces they need to fulfill the responsibilities of marriage.

Characteristics of Marriage

First, marriage is permanent, i.e. it is for life. No divorce and remarriage is permitted, as Jesus makes clear: "And I say to you, whoever divorces his wife, except for unchastity, and marries another commits adultery." (*Matthew* 19:1-9). The "unchastity" mentioned here (Greek, *porneia*) refers to incestuous unions which were therefore invalid from the start (Cf. John P. Meier, *Matthew* Wilmington Delaware 1986, p. 216). Although sometimes, sadly, couples do go through a civil divorce, perhaps because of physical abuse or some other serious reason, they remain married until death in the eyes of God. Hence, they are not free to marry someone else. The issue of a Decree of Annulment is discussed below.

Second, marriage is also exclusive. The two parties, this husband and this wife, belong exclusively to each other.

Third, marriage must remain open to life. This feature will be discussed further when we talk about the commandments.

*Fourth, m*arriage is between a man and a woman. In other words, it presupposes the complementarity of the sexes. Man and woman complete one another physically, emotionally and mentally, a fact that concerns not only the good of husband and wife but also that of the children. The Catholic Church therefore opposes the legalization of so-called "same-sex marriage." Our sex organs are clearly designed for procreation; homosexual actions are totally inconsistent with this natural order. Homosexuals may be friends but they cannot be marriage partners because they cannot perform marital acts.

Church Law Regarding Matrimony

Catholics are obliged to observe the form of marriage. In other words, they must enter into marriage in the presence of a priest and two witnesses, unless the bishop has granted a dispensation from this for some good reason. This requirement affects the validity of the marriage in the Catholic Church. A Catholic who attempts marriage with another person, Catholic or not, before someone other than a properly delegated Catholic priest, without a dispensation, is considered by the Church as not validly married.

There are various other impediments to marriage. For example, a Catholic requires a dispensation from mixed religion (or disparity of cult if the other party is not baptized) in order to enter into marriage with someone who is not a Catholic. In such mixed marriages, the Catholic party is required to promise that they will practise their faith and that they will do all in their power to see that any children born of the marriage are baptized and raised in the Catholic faith.

There are also impediments to marriage arising from consanguinity and affinity. Catholics may not marry within the first three degrees of consanguinity (second cousins). Civil law has similar prohibitions. Also, a person who has taken solemn vows, e.g. in a Religious Community, is not free to marry until they have been dispensed from their vows.

Of course, if one of the parties is a divorced person this is an obstacle to marriage in the Catholic Church unless that person has received a Declaration of Nullity in the Catholic Church.

What do we mean by a "Declaration of Nullity"? It is not "Catholic divorce," but a declaration by the Catholic Church, after thorough examination of the facts and proof supporting those facts that no valid marriage existed in the first place. For example, it might be established through the testimony of reliable witnesses that one of the parties entered into the marriage out of force or fear. (Think of a domineering parent who says, when their child expresses reservations about going ahead with the marriage, "You're not backing out of this marriage after all the money I've spent preparing for it, and you're not going to embarrass me in front of my friends by calling off this ceremony."). Another example might be the realization that one of the parties was incapable of the maturity required to give valid marriage consent. It might also be shown that one of the parties suffered from serious mental illness at the time of the marriage.

An application for Declaration of Nullity is made to the Diocesan Marriage Tribunal, which is staffed by people especially trained for this work. Obviously, it costs money to employ such people and to carry out the examination that is required. However, no application is ever refused because the person lacks the money to pay those costs. In such a case, if there are genuine grounds to go ahead with a marriage case and the person is truly unable to pay, it is recommended that the costs be paid out of parish funds.

This discussion of divorce and Declaration of Nullity helps us to appreciate better why the Catholic Church always requires a couple to take an approved Marriage Preparation Course before entering into marriage.

Sins Against Marriage

Adultery is obviously a grave sin against marriage. It represents a betrayal of one's solemn promise both to one's partner and to God. Yet the temptation to engage in adultery is always present, especially in today's culture. A simple piece of advice is the following. Keep close guard over your imagination, your fantasy world. This in turn demands that you exercise control over your glances, over the television programs you watch, and over your use of the internet.

Deliberate sterilization without a legitimate medical need (wherein the sterilization is indirect and unintended) is a serious sin against marriage because it takes away the openness to life that belongs to marriage, and because it attacks a healthy bodily organ.

Artificial birth control is opposed to Catholic teaching and to the total self-giving of marriage. In a later chapter, we will examine more closely what is wrong with artificial birth control, and will also consider natural family planning.

Helps for Marriage

• A good marriage preparation course. In 1986 a researcher in the Department of Sociology at the University of Western Ontario carried out a cross-Canada survey on marriage breakdown. The researcher discovered that the number one cause of marriage breakdown was "unreal expectations." A good course helps couples to be "more real" as they enter into their marriage.
• Marriage Encounter Weekends, and gatherings like Retrouvaille.
• Good counselling if difficulties arise.
• The fervent practice of your faith, and involvement in parish life. The statistics on how much of a difference this makes in marriage are startling.

Video

Your Marriage I (Liguori). All four parts of this video are excellent, but number I is especially inspiring and helpful.

Chapter 9

SACRAMENT OF THE SICK AND SACRAMENT OF HOLY ORDERS

There are three more sacraments yet to be considered. One of those sacraments, Confirmation, will be discussed in the final chapter. People who are completing an R.C.I.A, program, and are being received into the Church at the Easter Vigil, will receive this sacrament at that time, and it is appropriate to look at the meaning of this sacrament just before receiving it. For now, we will look at two sacraments: The Sacrament of the Sick and the Sacrament of Holy Orders.

The Sacrament of the Sick

This sacrament, along with the Sacrament of Reconciliation, is a sacrament of healing. It is conferred on people who are seriously ill. It continues the work of Jesus the Divine Physician, who healed sick people during his public life.

Times of illness and suffering can be frightening times, when we experience our frailty and glimpse death. They can lead to self-absorption, revolt, despair. However, they can also be occasions for us to become more mature, to acquire more empathy for others, to see what is really important in life, to identify with Christ in his sufferings for humanity, and so to come closer to God. Hence, these are times when we need God's assistance in a special way to reject negative attitudes and to adopt and live out positive, life-giving attitudes. Jesus gives us that assistance in the great Sacrament of the Sick.

Again and again in the Gospels, we see Jesus healing the sick, both in body and in spirit. It is the compassionate Lord reaching out. He did not, however, physically heal everyone. Those he did heal were a sign of the more fundamental healing he was bringing to the whole person, and to the entire human race.

Jesus associated his disciples with his work of healing. "He called the twelve and began to send them out two by two, and gave them authority over the unclean spirits ... They cast out many demons, and anointed with oil many who were sick and cured them" (Cf. *Mark* 6:7,13). Before his ascension, he commissioned his apostles to continue his work of healing: "And these signs will accompany those who believe: by using my name they will cast out demons; they will speak in new tongues; they will pick up snakes in their hands, and if they drink any deadly thing it will not hurt them; they will lay their hands on the sick, and they will recover." cf. *Mark* 16:17-18) The *Acts of the Apostles* shows Peter healing the sick (*Acts* 3:1-10).

The *Letter of James* bears witness to the early Church practice of the Sacrament of the Sick: "Are there any among you suffering? They should pray. Are they cheerful? They should sing songs of praise. Are any among you sick? They should call for the elders of the church and have them pray over them, anointing them with oil in the name of the Lord. The prayer of faith will save the sick, and the Lord will raise them up; and anyone who has committed sins will be forgiven" (*James* 5:13-15).

The Sacrament of the Sick is given by anointing the person on the forehead and hands with the Oil of the Sick (blessed by the bishop during Holy Week), and saying, *"Through this holy anointing may the Lord in his love and mercy help you with the grace of the Holy Spirit. May the Lord who frees you from sin save you and raise you up."*

This sacrament is given (a) to those who have a grave illness or injury, or (b) who suffer from frailty in old age, or (c) who are about to undergo a serious operation. The sacrament may be received again if the person experiences one of these situations again, or if a sick person's condition becomes more serious.

Only a priest or bishop confers this sacrament. It is important to call for a priest as soon as a person shows signs of truly serious illness or injury. The sacrament is usually preceded by the Sacrament of Reconciliation, the reading of the Word of God, praying over the person in the name of the Church, and laying of hands on the person's head.

The effects of this sacrament are:

(1) It brings about a strengthening, peace, and courage to deal with the illness, to trust in God, and to fight temptation. This is primarily a healing of the soul, but it sometimes also includes a healing of the body if that is God's

will.

(2) It promotes a union with the Passion of Christ. It is a kind of consecration, helping the sick person to unite their suffering to that of Christ for the redemption of the world.

(3) It causes a greater union with the whole Church, which prays for this person, who in turn offers their sufferings for the whole Church.

(4) It some cases the sacrament serves as a preparation for the person's final journey. If this is indeed the illness or injury leading to death, then this sacrament is a preparation for that final and most important time in life.

Holy Orders

Jesus, the Good Shepherd, also leads his people through earthly shepherds. From the Latin word for shepherd, these leaders are often referred to in our day as "pastors."

"The first Christians, while enjoying the basic equality of all the baptized and so sharing the same 'holy' or 'royal priesthood' (*I Peter* 2:5, 9), were, nevertheless, led and served by some who had performed specific ministries for them. We read that some received such ministries through the imposition of hands (e.g. *Acts* 6:6; *I Timothy* 4:14; *2 Timothy* 1:6) and we know the names for some office holders: *episcopoi* (overseers), *presbyteroi* (elders), and *diaconoi* (deacons). The development varied from place to place" (G. O'Collins, *Catholicism* Oxford 2003, p. 283).

Jesus had told the apostles at the Last Supper: "Do this in memory of me." The apostles followed this injunction of the Lord by celebrating the Eucharist. Later, when churches were established, they installed bishops in them to preside at the Eucharist. Those bishops later installed other bishops. Later on, the development of priests and deacons came about.

Important witnesses to this development are Clement of Rome (writing about A.D. 96), Ignatius of Antioch (writing about A.D. 110), Hippolytus, writing about A.D. 200).

The Sacrament of Holy Orders is conferred by the imposition of hands and the prayer of consecration offered by the bishop. A person can be ordained as bishop or priest only once and is marked forever thereafter as a bishop or priest. Deacons do not share in the ministerial priesthood but do receive the Sacrament of Holy Orders and are ordained by the bishop for a ministry of service.

Jesus is the only priest, the mediator between God and humans (cf. *Letter to the Hebrews*). However there are two kinds of sharing in that priesthood: First, the common priesthood of all the faithful: joined to Christ the priest by baptism all the faithful truly carry out priestly roles, by offering their daily life as a sacrifice joined to Christ's, by praying for the world, by offering Mass along with the priest, etc. Second, the ministerial priesthood: the special sacrament of Holy Orders joins the bishop or priest to Christ the priest in a special way; so Jesus exercises his office of head or shepherd visibly through them. Hence, the bishop or priest offers Mass, forgives sins in the Sacrament of Reconciliation, administers the Sacraments of the Sick and Confirmation.

The bishop, and in a lesser sense, the priest, is the spiritual leader of the Church-community. He co-ordinates, facilitates and encourages the gifts of the various members of the Body of Christ.

The bishop is the leader of the "local" Church-community, which is called a diocese (e.g. the Church of London, or Toronto, or Montreal, or Paris). The pope is the bishop of the Church of Rome. All other bishops must be in communion with him, though they have their episcopal powers and authority by reason of their ordination, and not by delegation from the pope (See *The Constitution on the Church*, no. 21).

The priest is the presence of the local bishop in a particular parish of the diocese; he is an extension of the bishop. Only the bishop is empowered to ordain other bishops and priests.

The permanent deacon is ordained as an assistant to the bishop and priests. He can preach, baptize, marry, bury, and generally instruct people, as well as ministering to the sick, etc. However, he is not empowered to say Mass, absolve from sins, or administer the Sacrament of the Sick.

Collegiality was an important truth emphasized by the Second Vatican Council. It means that the bishops together bear responsibility, in union with the pope, for the entire Church. This is why we have such events as Synods of Bishops, and General Councils of the Church.

Preparation for ordination is very important because of the great responsibility entrusted to the priest and bishop. Long years of training and education go into getting candidates ready for ordination. The seminary system, established by Council of Trent in the 16th century, is the usual means of training men for the priesthood today. Because the Church is human as well as divine, there are failures. However the vast majority of priests are faithful. One particular type of priestly failure that has been in the news in recent years is the sexual abuse of young people by priests. Horrible as such abuse is, it should be noted that figures from the Archdiocese of Washington show that only 2.5% of its priests in the fifty year period covering the last half of the 20th century were found guilty of such abuse. (*The Catholic Register*, Nov. 20/03). The average from most dioceses is estimated at 4%. Of course there are failures by priests in other ways as well, but, regrettable as these are, they should not distract us from the example given by the majority of faithful, caring priests.

There are different groups of priests: Diocesan priests are ordained to serve in a particular diocese, mostly in parishes but also in diocesan institutions like seminaries and church-run educational facilities. Religious priests are members of Religious Communities, dedicated to a particular type of apostolic work, like teaching, serving the sick, going out as missionaries, or leading a life of prayer on behalf of the entire Church.

Restriction to men: Only men can be validly ordained to the ministerial priesthood in the Catholic Church. It should be noted first that no one has a right to ordination (whereas baptism does confer on people a right to receive the Eucharist or the Sacrament of Matrimony, so long as they are properly disposed). The Church is free to choose those it decides to entrust with this responsibility. That means there is no social justice issue involved in denying the ministerial priesthood to women.

There is, however, a theological issue. It is the constant and unanimous teaching of the Church that Jesus chose only men for the college of twelve apostles, and that his successors did the same. Bishops and priests make that college of apostles present today. The Church believes therefore that Jesus himself made this decision, and that the Church is consequently not authorized to change it and ordain women. It should be noted that Jesus had a warm and inclusive attitude toward women in his ministry, and that he did not hesitate to go against many of the established customs of his society. Yet he freely and deliberately restricted the role of apostle to men. (Cf. Dulles, *The New World of Faith,* Huntington, Indiana 2000, p. 85-6. See also the excellent book on this topic by Sara Butler, *The Catholic Priesthood and Women: A Guide to the Teaching of the Church* Chicago 2007).

It is important to realize that the ordained priesthood is one form of service, and that women serve the Church in many crucial ways. Where would the Church have been, for example, without the service of the great Religious Communities of women responsible for Catholic schools and hospitals?

The question of authority and leadership is distinct from that of ordination to the ministerial priesthood. Increasingly today, women are occupying roles of authority and leadership in the church, though it is true that the Church has a long way to go yet in recognizing the special gifts of women by placing them in positions of leadership. (Cf. O'Collins, *op. cit.,* p. 389-90).

Celibacy is the way of life required for all Catholic bishops, and for Catholic priests of the Latin Rite. This is celibacy "for the sake of the Kingdom of God," and so it is something positive rather than just a restriction. It frees the priest's power to love so that love can be given unreservedly to the Lord and his people. Though this is purely Church law (and has been such for all priests of the Latin Rite since about the 11th century), and so could be changed, there are no signs that it is likely to be changed. There are exceptions to it though, and will continue to be. For example, non-Catholic Christian Pastors who are married men and become Catholic may be ordained as Catholic priests. Besides that, in several of the Eastern Rites of the Catholic Church a married man may be ordained to the priesthood (but not to the episcopate).

Many important Gospel values are embodied in this practice of priestly celibacy. First, consecration. The priest is consecrated, set aside, for God's purposes the way a chalice is, for example. Celibacy is a fitting sign in one who thus makes Christ the Pastor present. Second, spiritual marriage. The ministerial priest represents the Church, the Bride of Christ; his celibacy expresses that special intimacy or belonging to the Lord that is the feature of the bride. Third, celibacy involves an attitude of surrender, like the self-surrender of marriage. Fourth, celibacy is also a form of undividedness, in the sense of a total belonging to Christ and his people. Fifth, it is also a form of self-denial, an important Gospel value. Finally, priestly celibacy bears witness to belief in eternal life, since the priest does not have the kind of "immortality" that married people achieve through their children and grandchildren.

Video
    What Catholics Believe About the Sacraments (Liguori)

Appendix

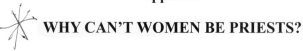

WHY CAN'T WOMEN BE PRIESTS?

The Official Position of the Catholic Church:

Ordinatio Sacerdotalis (issued by Pope John Paul II in May 1994): "In order that all doubt may be removed regarding a matter of great importance, a matter which pertains to the Church's divine constitution itself, in virtue of my ministry of confirming the brethren (cf. *Luke* 22:32) I declare that the Church has no authority whatsoever to confer priestly ordination on women and that this judgment is to be definitively held by all the Church's faithful." (Note how this is put: The Church does not have the "authority" to change this).

Is this an infallible teaching? The pope, as well as the Congregation for the Doctrine of the Faith (CDF), seem to have thought it was already infallible, but their judgment is not necessarily infallible.

We should notice that this is not a new issue. The question of women priests has been debated in the Patristic Age, in the Middle Ages, and in modern times. Almost without exception it has been answered in the negative.

Why Does the Catholic Church Hold This Position?

First, because Tradition, from earliest times, says it appears to be the will of Christ. If that is so then the Church clearly is not "authorized" to change it. How could you upset such a tradition with certainty (and you would need certainty)? We should note that this is also the unanimous teaching of the Orthodox Churches. Here is a quick overview of that tradition:

The New Testament – (1) Jesus treated women with respect but did not call them to be members of the Twelve. (2) Women clearly played an important role in the early Church, but the bishops and priests of the early Church, as we see it in the New Testament, were all men. (3) Several passages say women are excluded from ruling and teaching positions in the Church: *I Cor.* 14:34-35; *I Tim.* 2:12; *I Cor.* 14:37.

The Patristic Age – Several groups were judged to be heretical at least partly because they had women who sometimes celebrated the Eucharist. The Fathers of the Church unanimously opposed this practice.

The Middle Ages – (1) The Waldenses and the Cathari allowed women to be priests but the Church disapproved of this. (2) Hildegard of Bingen adamantly rejected the idea of women priests (and she was a feminist!). (3) The great medieval theologians argued strongly against the possibility of women priests.

The 19th Century – J.P. Migne, the great French Patrologist, whose collection of the Greek and Latin Fathers is still the definitive one, said that, based on his understanding of the Fathers, the teaching that women could be ordained priests, was heretical.

Second, because the argument which claims that the ban on women priests was purely a cultural one is not supported by the evidence. In other words, those people who say that Jesus did not include women in the Twelve because of the cultural climate of his time, are not being faithful to the picture of Jesus that we have from the Gospels. (1) Jesus had the greatest respect, care, love, and empathy for women, as so many Gospel passages show, yet he did not include them among the Twelve. (2) As Eric Mascall points out, it is ridiculous to suggest that Jesus was prepared to deprive women of their legitimate rights, and to mislead his Church on the true status of women, because he was afraid to go against the prejudices and conventions of his time. Even his enemies never accused him of being conventional or being guilty of cowardice. (3) Some people say that women would not have been accepted in a role of leadership because of the prejudices of the time. Yet priestesses and religions dominated by women were familiar to the people of Jesus' day. Moreover, the early Church was already so much in opposition to many of the established ways of Judaism and contemporary paganism that women priests would have been only a small addition to this opposition. (Think of Jesus' opposition to many of the pharisaic traditions, and the early Church's decision to admit Gentiles without making them become Jews, as well as the change of the Lord's Day from Saturday to Sunday, just to take a few examples).

Third, the theological reason most often advanced for this decision by Jesus is the so-called "iconic argument." Aquinas, Bonaventure and Duns Scotus all say that the priesthood is restricted to males because the priest represents Christ precisely in his capacity as the bridegroom of the Church, who offers the sacrifice that makes his beloved Bride holy. Dr. Marie Hendrickx, a theologian with the CDF, says, "From a deep, symbolic perspective, the masculinity of the priesthood and the magisterium is not insignificant. It is significant as representing the spousal relationship of Christ as Bridegroom, in love with the Church which is a feminine reality." This was also the teaching of the Council of Florence (1439) which said that the priest brings about the Eucharist by "speaking in the person of Christ." Pope Pius XII's 1947 *Mediator Dei* takes the same position, and so does Vatican II's *Lumen Gentium*, no. 10.

Other Important Considerations Regarding the Priesthood

First, we must never neglect the fact that all the baptized share in the common priesthood of the laity. In this wider sense, all baptized Christians are priests and share in the one priesthood of Jesus Christ. All the laity are a priestly people and carry out a priestly role in the Church and in society.

Second, the ministerial priest is not just a delegate of the congregation. He is ordained by the bishop, and thus receives powers that come from Christ.

Third, ordination to the ministerial priesthood is never anyone's "right." Therefore, there is no issue of justice involved here.

Other Important Considerations Regarding Women in the Church

First, there is a basic equality of men and women before God, and in the life of the Church. Along with this equality goes a diversity of roles.

Second, all of those roles that woman and men have in the Church are roles of service. The ministerial priesthood has to be seen as one of those forms of service. Moreover, we need to keep in mind that there are many roles of service, some of them more significant in some ways than the ministerial priesthood.

Third, the role and presence of women in all aspects of the Church's life has to be promoted much more. At the same time, much progress has been made in recent times. (1) Women today teach in theological colleges and seminaries. (2) Some women today are Chancellors of dioceses and Judges in Matrimonial Tribunals. (3) Many women today administer parishes where there is no resident priest. (4) Several important officials in the Vatican Curia are women. E.g. Professor Mary Ann Glendon and Dr. Marie Hendrickx. Still there is a long way to go.

Chapter 10

MID-POINT REVIEW AND TOUR OF CHURCH

For the benefit of those who may be using this book as a resource in conducting an R.C.I.A. program, or in giving someone instruction in the Catholic faith, this chapter provides for a "time out," a pause for reflection and prayer. It offers an outline for a brief review of what has been considered up to this point and a guide for a tour of the Church.

Review

Religion: fundamental to our lives; we are "tied" to God. Using our natural reason, we are led to the existence of God by both the world around us and the world within us. Natural religion is found in some form or other in every age and culture.

Revealed Religion – This is religion that results from God's initiative. In studying *Genesis*, especially from Chapter 12 onwards, we are struck by the fact that a lot of the people we meet are not good examples. Of course! God steps into the middle of human history, acting through the people he finds, like a good cook using leftovers. Yet what is remarkable is the hand of God guiding one tribe, Abraham's (1850 B.C.), to become a people worshipping the one God, and called to be a light to the nations. We see also the failures of this people to live up to their vocation; the prophets call them back, then speak finally of One who will himself fulfill the people's vocation – the "Anointed One," the Messiah or the Christ.

Christians – believe that Messiah or Christ is Jesus. We find the signs that confirm this belief, in his life, in his words, in his fulfillment of Old Testament expectation, in his miracles of mercy, and above all in his resurrection.

Record of this Revelation – The primary written record is called the Bible – 46 Old Testament books and 27 New Testament books. Sacred tradition, both oral and written, also provides a record for us. This revelation is communicated above all through the life of God's People, both before and after Christ. In 1850 B.C., God established a People; they wrote some books. In 30 A.D., Jesus established a People; they wrote some books. We Christians

92

need to keep in mind, however, that Jesus himself did not write a book; he established a Church. The Bible comes from the Church, not the other way around. In fact, the Bible as we know it today didn't exist as such until about 300 A.D.

Who is Jesus – First, he is the Messiah. Second, he is God the Son who took on our human nature (the most startling event in human history and the great truth of our faith). Third, he is the Redeemer, for Jesus opens again the way to eternal life.

Jesus Established the Church – He is present and active in the world through this Church, to which he is joined by the Holy Spirit, whom he sent on the Church at Pentecost. The Church-community is the Body of Christ, the presence and activity of Christ. That is why we speak of the infallibility of the Church.

The Sacraments – These are official acts of the Church, meetings with Christ. In the sacraments, Christ meets us to strengthen and help us.

Where is the Church? Full communion with the Church Jesus established requires: first, baptism; second, acceptance of all the teaching of Jesus and his Church; third, acceptance of the authority established by Jesus (Peter, whose successor today is the pope).

Rather than attempting a full review of the Eucharist, the Mass, Reconciliation and the other sacraments, it is probably more helpful here simply to see if there are any questions that inquirers have regarding these topics.

Where We Are Now

Christianity means following Christ, being attached to Christ. He is what the Catholic faith is all about. We must learn to have a personal relationship with him. We are to live as his disciples, a word that literally means, "learners." In succeeding chapters we will look in more detail at what such living involves.

At this point, however, inquirers into the Catholic faith should ask themselves: "What does all this mean for my life?" "Do I believe that the matters we have been considering are true?" (This is the only sufficient motive for becoming a Catholic.) Such questions also give emphasis to the importance of prayer in our life. We cannot know, or do, what is right without God's guidance. It is essential that we spend some quiet time in God's presence every day.

Tour of Church

There are *two* things we notice as soon as we enter the church. (a) We *bless ourselves* with holy water. This reflects the Jewish tradition of a symbolic washing at the door of Temple in order to come before God with sorrow for our sins and a desire to live a new life. The water in the holy water font is blessed water; it is a sacramental, and that means it has been blessed with a prayer asking God that those who use this water will be moved to sorrow for their sins and to a spirit of prayer. It is also a reminder of our Baptism, of who we are. (b) *We genuflect.* We do this to acknowledge the real Presence of Jesus in the Blessed Sacrament. Note the Sanctuary Lamp. In private visits to the church the Blessed Eucharist should be the focus of our attention.

The Sanctuary. Note the things that mark this as a Catholic Church: It has two foci: *altar and pulpit.* Jesus is present among us in Sacrament and in Word. In Protestant Churches that adhere to continental Reformation theology there would be only one focus point, the pulpit, Jesus present in his Word. Even the "Communion Services" celebrated sometimes in most Protestant Churches are intended only as symbols. (This is not the case however with many Anglican Churches and Lutheran Churches).

The Crucifix – It is prominent. The sign of defeat is really the sign of victory.

The Altar – The priests kisses it at the start of Mass (a) because the altar represents Christ, and (b) because of the ancient tradition by which there are relics of the martyrs in the altar stone (The Church no longer requires the presence of relics in the altar stone of new churches.) The Mass commits us to the kind of following of Christ that we witness in the martyrs.

The Easter Candle – Along with the other candles, it reminds us of Jesus, the light of the World. We, his Church, are called upon to let his light shine through us on our world. The Second Vatican Council's *Dogmatic Constitution on the Church* is entitled *"Lumen Gentium,"* "the light to the nations."

The Baptistry – This is the gateway to the Church; this joins us to Christ and to the rest of the Christian community. Methods of baptizing are by immersion and pouring.

The Stations of the Cross – "Station" is a stopping point on a journey (like a train station). The original "stations" are on the Via Crucis in Jerusalem, the route that tradition says Jesus took from the Praetorium to his place of execution on Golgotha. Stations of the Cross were originally outside the church, perhaps along a road, or in an enclosed area. Today in most cases, they are within the church itself. One walks from one station to the next, reflecting on what happened to Jesus at that particular point in his journey.

The Windows – Church windows traditionally contain scenes from the Bible. In the days when most people could not read, they were the ordinary person's catechism.

The Statues – As body-soul creatures we need images to focus our attention.

The Confessional Room

Video

Persons, Places and Practices in the Catholic Church (Liguori)

Chapter 11

THE CHRISTIAN LIFE – PART ONE

Christianity is not only a collection of truths to be believed, but is also a way of life to be lived. That way of life is portrayed for us in the Sermon on the Mount. When you read that sermon, in *Matthew* or *Luke*, your reaction might easily be, "Who in their right mind wants to live this way?" It seems to turn all sensible priorities upside down. Who wants to be poor, even "in spirit"? Who wants to "mourn"? Who feels like being "meek"? Then perhaps we say, "Well this sermon is just for certain people, people with a special call from God." But it is not. When we read the Gospel carefully, we see that this sermon is directed to all of us, to every Christian. It is a picture of Christian morality, a picture of what it means for anyone to live as a Christian, to have a Christian outlook, or to pursue a Christian lifestyle.

That in turn may lead us to say, "If the Christian life is that demanding, why try to live as a Christian?" The most obvious answer to that is because it is the truth. Jesus Christ truly is God who has come among us, for our sake, out of love for us. To follow him in our way of life is clearly to follow the path of truth.

Besides that, it is also clear that since God is our origin and our goal, God is our only true good. Therefore, to live in such a way that we can hope to spend eternity with God is the one good worth pursuing in life, no matter what the cost.

Thirdly, when we look at people who genuinely try to live the Christian life, they strike us as happy people. They possess a deep source of happiness that no difficulties seem able to shake. It is helpful to look closely at the lives of some of our modern saints, or candidates for sainthood, like Dorothy Day, or St. Damien De Veuster Yet even ordinary people we know who seriously try to follow Christ, strike us as happy people and as people who have a strong sense of meaning and purpose in life.

Christian morality can be expressed in four basic principles.

First Principle: "Become what you are"

The Christian life does not start with each of us striving to be good, and

God then rewarding us in some way for that. It starts with what God does for us. Through no merit of our own, simply by God's great goodness, we have been made sons and daughters of the Father in heaven through the sacrament of baptism. "See what love the Father has given us, that we should be called children of God, and that is what we are." (*I John* 3:1) So our call is to live like sons and daughters. Become what you are! "Christian, know your dignity" (St. Leo the Great). (See also *Ephesians* 5:1-5; *Philippians* 2:5-11). God first loved us and honoured us. Christian life responds to this. So the first principle of Christian morality is "become what you are." Moreover, it is God who makes our response possible. It is God alone who can and will transform us into true sons and daughters, if we are open to God's grace and co-operate with it.

Second Principle: "Live the Two Great Commandments"

What does it mean to live as a son or daughter of the Father? Jesus told an inquirer: Keep the commandments. However when asked what the greatest commandment was, Jesus replied: "You shall love the Lord your God with all your heart, and with all your soul, and with all your mind. This is the greatest and first commandment. And a second is like it: You shall love your neighbour as yourself. On these two commandments hang all the law and the prophets" (*Matthew* 22:37-39). We should note that last phrase. All the rest that God commands flows from these two commandments of love. So, the second principle of Christian morality is to become the kind of person who loves God above all things, and loves their neighbour as they love themselves.

The philosopher Henri Bergson (1859-1941) was not a Christian, but was a great admirer of some forms of Christian morality. He spoke of them as an "open morality" as opposed to a "closed morality." A closed morality is a morality of rules. If I do my duty and keep all the rules, I get one hundred! I'm perfect! God owes me! An open morality, however, is a call to love God, with all my heart, and to love my neighbour as myself. What I am called to here is a way of life that stretches far beyond anything I can become just by keeping some rules. I can never say I am good enough here, that I love God totally, or that I really love others just as greatly as I love myself. Each of us can see that we have miles and miles to go before we become this kind of loving person. Even though loving others does not necessarily mean liking them, we can see that it still means putting the needs and the good of others on the same level as my own.

Third Principle: "Become What You Were Created to Be"

It is clear, then, that Christian morality is not a matter of keeping a set of rules, but of becoming a particular kind of person. What kind of person? A loving person? Yes, but much more, a person who lives in accord with all the deeply human inclinations to truth and to goodness that an infinitely wise God has planted in us. Such a person strives with God's grace to perfect their distinctively human powers and so to develop the virtues. That person also comes to see that this pursuit of truth and goodness will only find its total fulfillment in the presence of God, the Supreme Truth and the Supreme Good, in the next life.

Of course, becoming this kind of person, someone who really begins to "flourish" as a human being, and who experiences the inner peace and happiness that accompany it, includes keeping the Ten Commandments. It would be totally dishonest to say that we loved God and our neighbour, and that we were seeking to become all that God meant a human to be, if we were not also doing our best to live according to the Ten Commandments. However, Jesus' words make it clear that being a Christian is not reducible to keeping the Ten Commandments. Being a Christian is primarily a matter of where our heart is. What are our priorities? What are our basic attitudes? The Ten Commandments are a kind of minimum morality, a set of wise guides to enable us to live together in peace while we are still in the early stages of virtue. Those who have developed the virtues, however, know what to do in each situation and they do it readily, even joyfully.

Fourth Principle: "Be Attentive to the Holy Spirit"

The beatitudes are the directions in which the Holy Spirit will lead a person of virtue. The Spirit leads them, in other words, in the footsteps of Christ. What do those directions involve? Here is how they are expressed in

Matthew 5: 1-12.

(1) *Blessed are the Poor in Spirit* - Our temptation is to think that money will make us happy. In part, this is the result of a shift in the 17th and 18th century, which resulted in money and possessions coming to be seen as an end rather than a means. The "poor in spirit" are people who see that these are only a means, and that they alone will not make us happy. Of course, we need money! There is nothing virtuous about being poor! However, the poor in spirit are those who come to see that our real joy comes from a living awareness that our lives are in the hands of a wise and loving God, and that we are carrying out our God-given role in God's world.

We are warned also that money and possessions are a danger! They can easily steal our heart. They can lead us to forget God, and to ignore the poor. If we concentrate on having money and things for ourselves, it will tend to close our heart.

(2) *Blessed are those who mourn* - It is important in life not to be fools. Fools are people who do not see what is going on around them. Those who mourn are people who do see what is happening in our world and in their lives. They are aware of the good in our world, but also of the power of evil in many social institutions and of the ways it touches their own life. Therefore, they are people who live with the truth, especially the truth about themselves. They are like the member of Alcoholics Anonymous who accepts the truth and has come to terms with it. This is a happy condition!

(3) *Blessed are the Meek* - It is so easy to misunderstand this beatitude. We think that the meek are wimps! That they are weak, passive people! We couldn't be more wrong! The meek are people of great courage. They are people who, each day, realize that they are in the hands of God's Providence. They accept that and are open to whatever that may bring. This attitude brings great inner peace and a wonderful sense of freedom to our lives. It also makes us caring and patient with others.

(4) *Blessed are Those who Hunger and Thirst for Righteousness* - The black civil rights leader, Jesse Jackson, once said: "When I pray 'Thy Kingdom come', I mean that Atlanta should look like heaven." To thirst for righteousness is to say the *Our Father* honestly. It is to want God's rule to

be accepted in every life and every social situation. Wherever that rule is accepted, life is much better. If God rules in our workplace or home, then that is a happy place because it's a place where everyone is being treated with respect and consideration.

(5) *Blessed are the Merciful* - All of us are tempted to turn in on ourselves, and just look after our own life. That quickly becomes a dead end. The "merciful" are people who honestly care about others, always, in every situation. They give others their full and undivided attention when they are with them. They care about the poor or needy (and people can be poor and needy in many ways). They also forgive others; they are not vengeful. Jesus says that, at the Judgment, God will care about them.

(6) *Blessed are the Pure of Heart* – The famous British politician, David Lloyd George once said, "The world stands aside for those who know where they are going." That is absolutely true! This is what we call single-mindedness. We call such single-mindedness purity of heart when people are focused above all on one thing each day: "What does God want of me? What is God asking of me this day, in this situation?" Before all else, I belong to God. This is the only attitude that will bring us real happiness. It will bring us ultimately the vision of God!

(7) *Blessed are the Peacemakers* - In the Bible, peacemaking is regarded as a truly great activity. The hymn we sing goes: "Let there be peace on earth and let it begin with me." Peace in our world begins with each of us making peace within our own personal relationships. The peace spoken of here is Shalom, that is, total well-being. What we work for is the well-being of others, of our home, our workplace, our neighbourhood and our community.

(8) *Blessed are you when you are persecuted for justice' sake* - All of us are conscious of peer pressure. We want to be accepted, to be part of the group. Fair enough! However, there are sinful forces in our society and in our personal world. So if we are trying to be faithful to Christ then there are going to be situations in which we will have to make choices. In such cases, others may ridicule us or give us a hard time because of our principles. Jesus says this is a good sign! It is a sign we are doing what is right! If this never happens to us, then we had better worry.

Self-Discipline

Living the Christian life calls for self-discipline. It is important to see here the difference between repression and suppression. The first is a form of hiding from the truth. The second is a training of our human powers so they can achieve their natural goals, like an athlete training for a contest. So we train ourselves to be patient, courageous, chaste, moderate in food and drink and so develop the virtues. The virtues bring our human powers to perfection. They make us more fully human, more completely alive. (cf. J. Dalrymple, *Theology and Spirituality* [Hales Corners, Wis. 1970] p. 66). So our morality is a virtue morality. It is not just about doing certain actions and avoiding others. It is about becoming a certain kind of person. Becoming that kind of person, with God's grace, involves an ongoing process of conversion.

Conversion

Acquiring the virtues and adopting the Christian attitudes that we call the beatitudes is the work of a lifetime. It is the process we call conversion. It is also a process that God brings about, not we ourselves, though God will not do it without our co-operation. It helps to surround ourselves with reminders of the kind of attitudes we are trying to acquire. We need to have a good crucifix, a Bible, sacred pictures, and stories or pictures of real heroes, those people who have truly lived the Christian life.

The Ten Commandments

We have said that living the Christian life includes, but is not reducible to, living the Ten Commandments. Here are some general observations about them.

They are not just arbitrary rules. They are a good presentation of what natural law requires of us. They are, in other words, what our nature cries out for. Behind each commandment is a good that God wants us to have. Live them and be more fully human.

We should also keep in mind the fact that the Ten Commandments were given to the people in the context of the covenant that God established with the Israelites, a covenant that was compared to a marriage ("I shall be your

God and you shall be my people"). The relationship with God was primary.

See *Psalm* 119 which expresses the Jewish love for the law of God and offers thanks for the wise guidance God provides us in that law.

In an appendix, we say something about the slightly differing order of these commandments as expressed by Catholics and Protestants.

Video:

The Ten Commandments for Teens. (Liguori). Though this video was designed for teenagers, it is so well done that adults find it helpful. Besides, people in the R.C.I.A. program often have children of their own and this video helps them to speak to their children about the commandments.

Appendix

ABBREVIATED LISTS OF THE TEN COMMANDMENTS

There are two lists of the Ten Commandments given in the Old Testament: *Exodus* 20: 1-17 and *Deuteronomy* 5: 6-21

The two lists differ from one another in several ways. The most important difference is that the list in *Deuteronomy* takes what is the 10th commandment in the *Exodus* list and appears to divide it into two commandments. In the *Exodus* list, one is forbidden to covet anything belonging to another. In the *Deuteronomy* list, one is forbidden to covet another's wife, and is forbidden to covet anything else "belonging" to another. Most scholars see here a development in moral awareness between the period of *Exodus* and that of *Deuteronomy*, so that people began to see one's wife as possessing a dignity that required speaking of her separately from the rest of a man's "possessions."

It has also been customary, from the time of the Israelite people, to recite abbreviated forms of the Ten Commandments. This would apply especially to abbreviating what appears in the first eleven verses of the *Exodus* account, and what appears in verses 6 to 15 of the *Deuteronomy* account. One of the practical reasons for such abbreviation would also be to deal with the fact that different reasons are given in the two accounts for keeping the Sabbath. The abbreviated accounts give no reason.

No one is sure exactly how the Jewish people abbreviated the Ten Commandments in the centuries before Christ.

Among Christians, two different abbreviated forms have been in use since the 4th century:

St. Augustine (354-430 A.D.), perhaps the most influential Christian writer of the early centuries, based his abbreviated list on the account in the *Book of Deuteronomy*. This involved dividing the commandment about "coveting" into two commandments, so that the 9th commandment became, "You shall not covet your neighbour's wife," and the 10th commandment became, "You shall not covet your neighbour's goods." In order to keep the total number of commandments at ten, St. Augustine then took *Exodus* 20: 2-6 to be represented by one commandment, "I am the Lord your God, you shall not have other gods before me." Some scholars think this may well have been the original form of the directives given in verses 1 to 6. Catholics and Lutherans have always followed the abbreviated list proposed by St. Augustine.

St. Jerome (347-419 A.D.), the best-known Biblical scholar of early Christianity, based his abbreviated list simply on the text in *Exodus*. This resulted in having only one commandment dealing with "coveting," the tenth commandment, which forbade the coveting of anything of another's, including one's wife. It also involved making the words "You shall not make for yourself an idol (or graven image)" the second commandment, distinct from what is given in verse 2, "I am the Lord your God, you shall have no other gods before me," which remains the first commandment in both lists. The Orthodox Churches, present day Jews, and most Protestants, follow this list.

In practice, the two lists cover the same ground, though what is called second, third, fourth, etc. differs in the two lists. The only issue one might raise is that concerning the making of graven images, which appears in St. Jerome's list but not in St. Augustine's. Does this prohibition need to be made explicit? Most scholars agree that these words forbade only making images of Yahweh (God). God, after all, ordered his people to make certain other images (the bronze serpent, the cherubim over the Ark of the Covenant). In 787 A.D., the 7th General Council of the Church, meeting at Nicaea, justified the use of icons or images of Christ, Mary, the angels, and the saints. Such images are "venerated," not worshipped as God alone is.

The Catechism of the Catholic Church uses *Exodus* 20:2-5 for the first commandment.

References:

The New Catholic Encyclopedia, Vol. 4, article on "The Ten Commandments."

The New Jerome Biblical Commentary, comments on the *Book of Exodus*.
The Catechism of the Catholic Church

Chapter 12

THE CHRISTIAN LIFE – PART TWO

Introductory Notions

Conscience – When it comes to deciding how we should act in particular situations, we turn to our conscience. What does it tell us we should do? Conscience, however, is not an independent source of moral knowledge; it is not some kind of inborn encyclopedia of morality. It is an act of judgment made by our practical reason, applying the moral knowledge we have acquired, to some present circumstances. Clearly, then, it is dependent on the quality of the moral knowledge we have received from various sources, including the teaching of the Church. We have a duty, then, to see that our conscience is rightly informed. Hence the importance of what we are about to do in considering Catholic moral teaching.

Mortal and Venial Sin – This traditional distinction is reaffirmed by Pope John Paul II in his 1993 document, *The Splendour of Truth*. See also *I John* 5:16-17: "If you see your brother or sister committing what is not a mortal sin, you will ask, and God will give life to such a one – to those whose sin is not mortal. There is sin that is mortal; I do not say that you should pray about that. All wrongdoing is sin, but there is sin that is not mortal." Mortal sin ("*mors*" means "death") breaks our relationship with God. There are three conditions for it: serious matter; full knowledge; full consent. If we die in a state of mortal sin, we go to hell. Hell means to be eternally in the state of separation from God that we were in at the moment of our death. Venial sin is to be fought against, especially through such remedies as frequent confession. Note here the role played by temptation and the occasions of sin, especially in our present-day society.

Occasions of sin – What could lead us into sin. So far as possible, we have a duty to avoid such occasions.

First Commandment: "I am the Lord your God: you shall not have strange gods before me."

This is a call to seek out the truth about God and live in accord with it.

It is also a call to live in such a way that we see God as our supreme good.

Do not "genuflect to the world," as the great Catholic philosopher Jacques Maritain once said. Do not let anything else take the place of God in our life.

It is also a call to pray, privately and publicly. We are body-soul creatures and we are also social creatures; our prayer needs to respect all these aspects of our human existence.

This commandment also calls us to worship God by carrying out faithfully our role in caring for this world and serving human society's needs. We and we alone on this earth are the "images of God," called to manage and develop this world on God's behalf.

We fail in our worship of the true God if we indulge in superstition or magic. We also sin if we deliberately doubt the truths that God teaches us through his Church. All people have difficulties at times with some of the truths of their faith, but a difficulty is not the same thing as a doubt. We do need to grow in our knowledge and understanding of our faith just as we seek to grow in other areas of human knowledge.

Second Commandment: "You shall not take the name of the Lord your God in vain."

Our power of speech, the power to communicate with others using verbal symbols, is a great gift. We should respect it and use it at all times in the way that human reason demands. Clearly, this is an area in which we need to exercise a good deal of self-discipline. Cf. *James 3:1-12:* "Anyone who makes no mistakes in speaking is perfect, able to keep the whole body in check with a bridle ... From the same mouth come blessing and cursing. My brothers and sisters, this ought not to be so."

Some people do indulge in vulgar language, including the misuse of God's Name. When this occurs as a result of habit, it is not a serious sin. However, there is a responsibility to take the steps needed to overcome the habit. We should also be conscious of the kind of social atmosphere we help create by the language we use.

This commandment especially calls on us never to invoke the Name of God in support of a lie (perjury); never to harm other people in the name of God; never to use expressions insulting to God or religion.

The best way to observe this commandment is to use God's Name in a positive way; praise God, thank God; make God our companion every day by turning to God in moments of personal prayer; ask for God's help in various situations. Silently say a prayer blessing God whenever we hear anyone else using the name of God or Jesus in vain. Consider the power of the name of Jesus, used by Peter in the *Acts of the Apostles* to cure people. Let our reverence for God's holy name be an act of humility, showing that we do not know the mysterious Mind of God.

Third Commandment: "Remember to keep holy the Sabbath Day."

The Sabbath for the Jewish people was Saturday. Christians changed the day to Sunday, because Jesus rose on the first day of the week, and because Christians needed to distinguish themselves from other Jews. (Cf. *Acts 11:25*).

To participate in Sunday Mass (or in the Saturday evening Vigil Mass) is a serious obligation. To be a Christian means to be part of the Community of Faith and to offer the Eucharist with it. One should never miss Sunday Mass except for a serious reason, such as illness or caring for the sick. Sometimes today, people are required by their employment to work on Sunday; if they have no choice then this is not their fault. However often they can assist at the Saturday Vigil Mass. We need the support of others in our faith, and they need us.

As much as possible we should also observe Sunday as a day of rest. We need to use it as a day to celebrate those things that do not come from human effort but are simply the gift of God. Beware of becoming a slave of work! Make Sunday a family day, and refrain from shopping on Sunday.

Fourth Commandment: "Honour your father and your mother."

This commandment obviously concerns the mutual responsibilities of parents and children. Children, especially as they grow older, should show their parents a realistic, forgiving, grateful love; we do not love our parents because they are perfect but because they are our parents. It is important for parents and children to keep open the lines of communication at all times.

We are also required to respect other legitimate authority, and to see all such authority as coming from God. We have a serious responsibility to obey all just laws, including traffic laws, and to pay our taxes.

This commandment reminds us of the dignity of politics. Pope Pius XI spoke of political charity (exercised, for example, by a willingness to serve in public office) as one of highest forms of charity. We have a responsibility to be politically informed and to vote conscientiously. We should also be ready to run for public office if we have the necessary qualifications

Fifth Commandment: "You shall not kill."

God is the Master of life – Every human being is made in the image of God, is deeply loved by God, and was redeemed by Christ. Hence, we must respect the life of every human being at every stage of existence, from conception to natural death. Thus abortion and euthanasia are wrong, but so also are other attacks on human life such as deliberately neglecting the poor, the unemployed and the refugee, e.g. by the political policies we support.

This commandment forbids murder, suicide, doing physical harm to other people, hatred, and a spirit of revenge.

Direct sterilization and any other attack on a healthy physical organ or power without a therapeutic medical reason is wrong.

Abusing alcoholic drink or drugs is condemned because it is contrary to our responsibility to care for our health.

This commandment forbids drinking and driving, as well as other forms of reckless driving.

Anger and verbal abuse as well as putting other people down are contrary to this commandment. Karl Marx referred to speech as a "weapon."

What about our duty to preserve our life? What remedies are we required to take when we are seriously ill? We must use all ordinary means to preserve our life, but are not required to use extraordinary means. For example, if I have incurable cancer I am not obliged to take chemotherapy.

What about war and capital punishment? See treatment of these questions in the appendices.

We are reminded by this commandment that forgiveness is essential to a Christian.

Sixth Commandment: "You shall not commit adultery"

Sex is a marvellous power and gift from God. Its primary purpose is to give human beings a share in God's own joyful creative activity. Therefore, it carries with it a great responsibility.

Sex is something profoundly serious. Several recent writers have pointed out that the great mistake of our culture is to reduce sex to something trivial. Many years ago, a Catholic philosopher, Dietrich von Hildebrand, wrote a book entitled *In Defence of Purity*. One of the points he makes in this thoughtful study is that our sexuality reaches to the very depths of our being. There is a centrality to sex; my sexuality is profoundly me.

Sex is a social power; it is not just for oneself. Though it is legitimate to do many other things alone, it is wrong to reduce sex to something solitary. Sexual intimacy with another, because of the centrality of sex, represents the total gift of self. For this reason, it belongs only within a committed, lifelong, exclusive heterosexual marriage. Sex between a man and woman who are not married to one another is a lie. It says, "I give my entire self to you," while at the same time withholding that total gift.

It is also the lifelong commitment of marriage that sustains genuine sexual love. The Lutheran theologian, Dietrich Bonhoeffer once gave this advice to a young couple: "Today you are young and very much in love and you think that your love can sustain your marriage. It cannot. Let your marriage sustain your love."

The Catholic Church's teaching on sex is a positive one, emphasizing the greatness and seriousness of our sexuality. Today that teaching has to face a shallow social climate that works against it. We do great good, not just to ourselves but also to our society by being chaste and modest in a healthy way.

Sins against our sexuality include adultery (where at least one of the parties is married to someone else); fornication (where neither party is married); masturbation (solitary engagement in sexual activity), homosexual activity (While there is nothing sinful about having a homosexual inclination, sexual activity with another person of one's own gender is morally wrong). All such sins are, of their nature, serious.

Indulging in pornography and frequenting immodest movies or shows degrades people, trivializes sexuality, and harms our ability to relate in a wholesome way to other people.

Artificial birth control is a serious sin against marriage. The reasons why the Church condemns artificial contraception are dealt with in an appendix to this chapter. A video on natural family planning can also be shown later.

Eighth Commandment: "You shall not bear false witness against your neighbour"

This commandment reminds us that, as humans, blessed with the ability to know and understand, we need to cultivate a love for the truth. The search for truth is a search for God. Faithfulness to the truth is important to our personal integrity. We hurt ourselves when we lie. We even start to believe in our lies and so to live in a false world. Of course, fidelity to truth is also the basis for life with others in a spirit of trust and reliability.

The eighth commandment forbids deliberate lies, detraction (telling other people's faults without necessity), calumny (telling lies about other people), and rash judgment (judging others without sufficient evidence).

We are not obliged, however, to tell everything to everyone. There are situations in which we may, and often should, avoid revealing the truth to another, though we may never indulge in a deliberate lie to do this.

We are also obligated to keep secrets: when our professional relationship to others requires it; when we have promised to do so; when others have a right to expect that we will do so.

Ninth Commandment: "You shall not covet your neighbour's wife"

Actions against the sixth commandment often find their origin in improper sexual thoughts and desires. Jesus spoke of "committing adultery in the heart." Hence, it is wrong to indulge willfully in impure thoughts and desires. The word "willful" is important here; everyone has temptations, but the person of virtue turns away from them.

Modesty in action, dress, and speech is important to guard against improper thoughts or desires.

Tenth Commandment: "You shall not covet your neighbour's goods"

Envy at the sight of another's earthly goods is wrong and can lead to the temptation to steal.

Such envy can also engender an immoderate desire to possess earthly goods. In this sense, the tenth commandment is a particularly important one in our culture where we are surrounded by enticements to consumerism. This is at the root of actions that lead people into too much debt, and into working immoderately (sometimes in more than one job) simply out of a spirit of greed.

The Virtues

We have referred to the virtues, which perfect our human powers. To have the virtue of truthfulness, for example, is to be a person who has developed their love for the truth in such a way that they always, and easily, tell the truth. They have become a truthful person. St. Thomas Aquinas tells us: "We become the choices we make." There are two kinds of virtues:

First, there are the natural virtues. They perfect our natural powers. There are four principal (cardinal = hinge) ones: prudence (good sense), justice, temperance (self-discipline) and fortitude (courage). All the other natural virtues fit under these headings. Prudence perfects our practical reason, justice our will, temperance our concupiscible appetites, and fortitude our irascible appetites.

Second, there are the theological virtues. These are infused virtues (not acquired) and are given to us by God along with the sacrament of Baptism. These are faith, hope, and charity. They give us the radical power to participate in God's own life. We should learn acts of faith, hope, and charity and recite them often. These virtues give shape to our entire life, and affect our natural virtues, giving them a new direction in many situations.

God's grace, supported by our goodwill and effort, should make us virtuous persons. In this, Jesus is our model, the perfect human.

Video

Natural Family Planning: An Alternative for You. (Sheed and Ward LL8392)

Appendix I

CATHOLIC TEACHING ON ARTIFICIAL CONTRACEPTION

The Church teaches that, to respect the two purposes of marriage and the act that expresses it, every sexual act should express committed love and at the same time be open to the possibility of procreation.

So the Church has always taught, and clarified most controversially in the Encyclical *"Humanae Vitae"*, that it is morally wrong to destroy the sexual act's capacity for giving life either permanently through sterilization or temporarily through contraception.

To begin, it would be good to clear up some typical misunderstandings about this:

First, that the Church expects couples to have as many children as possible. This is not true. While the Church promotes generosity in the service of life, the Church advocates responsible parenthood as well and has never taught that spouses should have more children than they can handle, physically, emotionally or financially.

Second, that the Church opposes contraception because it is artificial. This is far from true. If that were true, the Church long ago would have also condemned other artificial things, all the way from aspirins and hearing aids to artificial limbs.

The problem is not the artificial means that a contraceptive involves, it is that a contraceptive device destroys or interferes with our natural life-giving capacity. Other artificial things like aspirins and eyeglasses help restore our natural capacities or return them to natural functioning.

Third, that contraceptives are morally equivalent to other methods like natural family planning methods because they both have the same goal – preventing a pregnancy. But the difference is in the means we choose to the end. One is legitimate because it does not remove or interfere with our natural life-giving potential, the other however does.

So why basically is the use of a contraceptive wrong? As Pope Paul VI expressed it:

112

1. It violates natural law. That is to understand we can discern in the nature of the sex act itself that it has procreation as one of its given purposes. Our nature or natural capacities indicate to us the intention of their Creator, and so to violate this nature or natural capacity is to violate the intention of the Creator. True enough, a woman is not fertile anyway for a good part of her cycle, but there is a moral difference between respecting that God-given fertility and altering it to suit our purposes.

2. To justify contraception would lead to a slippery slope of justifying or begetting other moral evils.

- Governments forcing contraception on their people to attain desirable social goals.
- Abortion as the last-ditch contraceptive.
- Increased marital infidelity.
- More sexual experimentation and promiscuity among young people.
- Homosexual unions seen as equivalent to heterosexual in that procreation would be eliminated as an essential purpose of the sexual act.

It would be hard to argue that we have not seen such things come about since 1968.

3. Later on Pope John Paul II would say that it violates the total self-giving that the sexual act is supposed to express. So that instead of giving all of myself, I give you only a part, with the life-giving part of myself held back or suppressed.

A few words are in order now about responsible parenthood and family planning in Christian marriage. Fortunately, couples need not be left between a rock and a hard place, because there is a method of family planning that is morally acceptable and effective.

It's a form of natural family planning that has often gone by the name of the ovulation or Billings method. It is not the old calendar rhythm method, based on a woman's menstrual cycle, but is based on physiological changes in a woman at the time of ovulation. If applied correctly, the World Health Organization has determined that it is over 98% effective, and that it is just as effective as the pill.

Besides being a method that respects God-given fertility and the life-giving capacity of the act, couples who have tried it have really become strong advocates of the method in view of the fact that it has enhanced both their sense of dignity and even their relationship as a couple in a number of ways. First, it does not involve any device or any of the health risks posed by other means. Second, it has deepened the level of communication between the couple. Third, during the 6 to 9 days each month of the fertile period, couples have been able to rediscover and enhance the romance of their marriage by showing affection for one another in other physical and non-physical ways. Fourth, women have found that their partners, in respecting their fertility, respect them more. There is far less likelihood of them being treated as objects always available for satisfaction.

Appendix II

THE JUST WAR

Possible Positions on War

1. Militarism – War is seen as inevitable, a natural expression of human aggressive instincts. There is a new kind of militarism in fundamentalist views of war as God's punishment on our world.

2. The Just War – Some wars, under certain conditions, are justified.

3. Pacifism – Violence and bloodshed are so wrong in themselves, that to use them even for defence, is to use an evil means for a good end.

The Catholic Teaching on Just War

The first writer to speak on the morality of war was St. Augustine (5th century). His ideas were developed by St. Thomas Aquinas (13th century) and by writers like Vitoria, Suarez and Bellarmine (16th century). The following conditions are required for a war to be considered just:

1. It must be conducted by a lawful authority.

2. It must be carried on for a just cause.

- There must be sufficient proportion between the good to be accomplished and the accompanying evil.
- War must be the last resort
- There must be a fair hope of success

3. It must be conducted with a right intention.

4. It must employ just means:

- The purpose of a just war is to put the enemy's war machine out of commission. This will normally include the killing of some soldiers.
- The principle of discrimination must be respected: One must not attack non-combatants (though this distinction is hard to apply at times).
- Proportionality must be observed in the choice of weapons, etc. (The harm done must not be out of proportion to the good to be hoped for).
- International agreements on treatment of prisoners, etc. are to be respected.

The first three conditions are usually spoken of as involving *jus ad bellum.* The fourth condition is spoken of as concerning *jus in bello.*

Recent Catholic Teaching on War

There is an extensive treatment of the subject of war in Vatican II's *Constitution on the Church in the Modern World*, numbers 79-82. The following words are especially significant:

"Any act of war aimed indiscriminately at the destruction of entire cities or extensive areas along with their population is a crime against God and man himself. It merits unequivocal and unhesitating condemnation." (no. 80)

In the light of this pronouncement, many national conferences of Catholic Bishops, and leading Catholic theologians, teach that the use of nuclear weapons can never be morally justified under any circumstances. Moreover, many Catholic theologians believe that a logical consequence of this position is that it is immoral even to maintain nuclear weapons as a threat to other nations. The policy of "nuclear deterrence," they believe, cannot be justified morally. Nations have an obligation to move away from it. Increasingly this has been the position found in official Catholic documents.

Appendix III

CAPITAL PUNISHMENT

Teaching of St. Thomas Aquinas

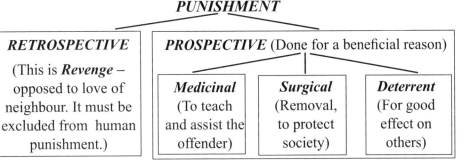

PUNISHMENT

RETROSPECTIVE (This is *Revenge* – opposed to love of neighbour. It must be excluded from human punishment.)	*PROSPECTIVE* (Done for a beneficial reason)		
	Medicinal (To teach and assist the offender)	*Surgical* (Removal, to protect society)	*Deterrent* (For good effect on others)

Teaching of the Catholic Church

"This is the context in which to place the problem of the death penalty. On this matter, there is a growing tendency, both in the Church and in civil society, to demand that it be applied in a very limited way or even that it be abolished completely. The problem must be viewed in the context of a system of penal justice ever more in line with human dignity and thus, in the end, with God's plan for man and society. The primary purpose of the punishment which society inflicts is 'to redress the disorder caused by the offence.' Public authority must redress the violation of personal and social rights by imposing on the offender an adequate punishment for the crime, as a condition for the offender to regain the exercise of his or her freedom. In this way, authority also fulfills the purpose of defending public order and ensuring people's safety, while at the same time offering the offender an incentive and help to change his or her behaviour and be rehabilitated.

"It is clear that, for these purposes to be achieved, the nature and extent of the punishment must be carefully evaluated and decided upon, and ought not to go to the extreme of executing the offender except in cases of absolute necessity: in other words, when it would not be possible otherwise to defend society. Today, however, as a result of steady improvements in the organization of the penal system, such cases are very rare, if not practically non-existent." Pope John Paul II, *The Gospel of Life* (1995) no. 56.

 Teaching of the Canadian Catholic Bishops

March 1976: they passed a resolution favouring abolition of the death penalty. They spoke of this as an action taken out of respect for life, seeing the death penalty as a violent measure that begets violence.

Position of Major Churches in Canada

There was an Interchurch Taskforce on Alternatives to the Death Penalty, which prepared a packet of information for each legislator when capital punishment was being debated in 1976. Capital punishment was opposed by the Catholic Church, the Anglican Church, the United Church of Canada, the Presbyterian Church, the Baptist Church, the Lutheran Church, the Unitarian Church, the Mennonite Church, the Quakers, and the Central Conference of American Rabbis.

Historical Development of the Issue

Since 1750, there has been a gradual movement against the death penalty, especially for three reasons:

1. It is needlessly cruel, especially if a society is going to value life.
2. It is over-rated as a deterrent.
3. It is occasionally imposed in fatal error.

The reason most often given for the death penalty is that its existence deters violent crime. Studies do not support this. In Canada, capital punishment was suspended in practice in 1963; and legally abolished in 1976.

Chapter 13

THE SOCIAL TEACHING OF THE CHURCH

In speaking of the Sacrament of Matrimony, we called attention to the intriguing event reported near the beginning of St. John's Gospel when Jesus changed ordinary water into very good wine at a marriage feast (2: 1-11). St. John concludes the account with the words: "Jesus did this, the first of his signs, in Cana of Galilee, and revealed his glory, and his disciples believed in him." John calls this a "sign" because it shows what Jesus' ministry is all about. Jesus has come to change everything, to make everything new. He will go on to change sick people into healthy ones, and even dead people into living ones. This means Jesus has come to transform all social institutions. We have already mentioned this in regard to his change of marriage into a sacrament. Catholic social teaching is about the ways in which all our economic, social and political institutions are to be transformed by the power of the Gospel.

The Seventh Commandment: "You shall not steal"

The seventh commandment is rooted in the right to private property. The Church does defend this as a legitimate right; hence the duty we have of respecting the property of others, and also the requirement of restitution if we steal from another or willfully damage the property of others. At the same time, consideration of this commandment leads us quite naturally into a discussion of the Social Teaching of the Church.

The Social Teaching of the Catholic Church on Property

The notion of property – We should begin by noting that there is a fundamental sense in which all property is common. We mean by this that no one's name is written by nature on any part of this earth. In this sense, God is the only owner of the whole earth. It is all his "property." As the "owner," God has made us the stewards or managers of his property. The Book of *Genesis* says that we are made in the "image of God." "Let us make humankind in our image, according to our likeness; and let them have

119

dominion over the fish of the sea, and over the birds of the air, and over the cattle, and over every creeping thing that creeps upon the earth" (1:26). These words mean that humans are somewhat like God in the sense that they are self-directed, and therefore capable of managing things. For that reason, God gives humans the following commission: "Fill the earth and subdue it; and have dominion over the fish of the sea and over the birds of the air" (1: 28). Humans are God's managers and therefore answerable to God for how they carry out this responsibility.

In light of this fact, we can make the following assertion: All humans have a natural right to take part in this vocation to manage, care for, and make human use of the world. This is the fundamental right to property that all humans have by nature.

Private property – Experience shows, however, that the only workable way of managing this world responsibly is by setting up some system of private property. This is because of human weakness and sinfulness. For example, when things are held in common, the situation tends to give rise to quarrels. Besides that, things held in common tend to be treated more carelessly. This argument goes all the way back to Aristotle, who points out that a system of private ownership results in the goods of this earth being handled in a way that is (a) more careful, (b) more orderly, and (c) more peaceful. It is on these "existential" grounds that humans, as we know them, usually require a system of private ownership in order to carry out their role of acting as God's images in caring for this world in a manner that is efficient and peaceful. That is why the Catholic Church defends the principle of private property and speaks of humans as having a right to private property.

At the same time, any particular system of private property-holding that seriously interferes with the more fundamental right of every person, as an image of God, to share in the management, development and human use of the goods of this world is unjust. Thus a system so constructed that private ownership of 90% of a country's arable land remains in the hands of just a handful of rich families, a situation that has arisen in some countries, is completely unjust. So too is any system of private property that allows huge areas of arable land to be left idle while people are unable to provide the necessities of life for their families. Many today question a system in which the poor keep getting poorer and the rich keep getting richer.

Ownership is an analogical term – The use of private property often has serious impact on other people. The less directly something I privately own is related to my person, the more I must take into account the social character of my property-holding. For example, my clothes are exclusively mine. However, my automobile is much more a social entity affecting other people. This is the basis for limitations on the way I use it, and for the right of others to use it in emergencies. My investments, like stocks and bonds can have a great social impact. Hence, I must use them only in ways that do not harm, but that help others, including the poor.

Ownership is a means – Possession is not an end in itself (though the "consumerist" mentality of our culture subtly preaches that it is). Human fulfillment does not come from what we have but from what we are. Ownership is, instead, a means to protect and enhance human dignity. We own things so that we can carry out our role of acting as the images of God in our management and use of the goods of this world. It is the faithful carrying out of our vocation or calling in life that brings us fulfillment, not the earthly goods we possess to help us in this endeavour.

The Use of Property – Since God is the only real owner of this world's goods, and we humans are only stewards or managers, there are four principles that we need to keep in mind in our use of earthly goods:

(a) The Principle of Involvement – I am entitled to seek possession of those goods that I need to carry out the duties of my state in life. Obviously, this also means that a married person with a family needs more. Therefore, in seeking to possess or accumulate, we should look at our needs, not our wants.

(b) The Principle of Stewardship – We cannot separate ownership from responsibility. We are answerable to God for how we manage and use the goods in our care, and must be attentive to the social impact of what we own.

(c) The Principle of Detachment – Money and possessions are a danger to us. We can become so attached to them that we lose our "taste" for God. We can also become so taken up with them that we sacrifice more important goods, like the needs of the poor, to our quest for possession.

(d) The Principle of Witness – Our lives are meant to announce the Gospel. We preach much more by what we are and how we live than by what we say. Our possession and use of earthly goods should show that we truly believe in eternal life. They should also show that we are aware of the fact that we live in a world of poor people and that we must care about them as we care about ourselves.

Investments – Today many people in our economy eventually invest some of their money in stocks or bonds. When we invest in a stock, we become a part owner of the corporation in which we have invested. That means we share responsibility for how that corporation acts in our society. It is immoral simply to collect dividends and to distance oneself from how those dividends are being earned. When we invest in a bond, we do not become owners but we lend money to a corporation. Even here, we should look carefully at what we are supporting by that loan. Mutual funds are difficult to defend from a moral point of view because we do not know what we are investing in. Such funds tend to separate ownership from responsibility, something that is always immoral.

How we spend our money – We "vote" with our money in the sense that we support certain businesses when we buy their products or services. Therefore, we need to look at the social effects of where we shop and what we buy. What are we supporting by our use of our money? What about buying products made by child labour, by people toiling in sweatshop conditions in poor countries; or produced by prisoners in China? What about giving our business to stores in our country that pay low wages, are hard on their employees, and are fiercely anti-union?

Some Other Basic Principles of Catholic Social Teaching

The dignity of the person – What makes human beings truly distinctive among all other animals on this earth is the fact that they can know God. It is when evolution reached that point at which human beings could appear that, for the first time, nature was able to recognize and acknowledge the God from which it came. Humans are nature's voice and nature's hands in responding to the God of creation.

As we have seen, the *Book of Genesis* (1:26) also pictures humans as being like God because they are capable of taking responsibility for their actions. We recognize this aspect of their dignity by referring to humans as "subjects."

Besides that, God the Son took on our human nature and lived among us to redeem us. In so doing, Jesus identified himself with every single other human and so gave to every human being a value and importance far surpassing any other created thing on this earth.

Because of their dignity, humans also have natural rights. A natural human right is an entitlement to whatever we need as humans in order to become what God has called us to be. (It is not, then, an entitlement to whatever we happen to seek as a form of self-expression). We have self-executory rights, that is, civil and political rights, like the right to life, liberty, freedom of expression, the right to engage in business, etc. Such rights are the kind that we are able to exercise so long as no one interferes. We also have programmatic rights, that is, social and cultural rights, such as the right to employment or to a guaranteed level of income. Rights of this kind require the presence of social and political institutions in our society to guarantee them.

Only humans are "subjects." It is wrong to treat them as mere objects (as so many of our economic structures do). Humans have the right to be actively involved in the various social, political, or economic institutions of which they are a part.

The social nature of the person – We are not just individuals. We are social beings. We define ourselves by the communities of which we are part and to which, therefore, we have responsibilities (our family, our ethnic community, our nation). This leads to two other principles: (a) *The Principle of Solidarity*, which means that society is something like a family. This is why we defend universal social programs, like old age pension or health care, to which each of us is entitled simply because we are part of the "family." (b) *The Principle of Subsidiarity* which means that society is something like the human body, in the sense that it has, within it, "lower" societies to carry out its various functions, as a body uses eyes for seeing and feet for walking.

Such "lower" societies are the family, civic organizations, labour unions, etc. A healthy society has many such "intermediary groups." It also respects and supports their activity without attempting to take it over.

The common good – This is the good we get by being part of some group and only by being part of that group. Think of the good we get by being part of a free society, or the good we get by being part of a winning hockey team. In each case, it is a good that requires us to contribute our share and to follow certain rules. Yet in return, we receive a great good we would not have otherwise. Hence, we need to be conscious of the common good. The enemy of the common good is the purely private good, that is, "my" profit, "my" career, "my" glory, which can so occupy us that we ignore our primary duty to promote the common good.

Human work – Since we have been created in the image of God, the work each of us does is our particular role in managing and developing the world that God has entrusted to humanity's care. So we need to see what we do each day, not just as a job (a means to make money or to get some economic service performed), not just as a career (a means to satisfy our personal ambition), but above all as a calling.

Labour unions – The right and indeed the need, for these organizations is based on (a) the fact that human persons are subjects, not just objects, and so have a right to a say in the conditions of their employment; (b) the principle of subsidiarity, which demands that working-people speak and act in their own name rather than being dependent on some form of "paternalism;" (c) the dignity of human work, which demands that wages and conditions be worthy of human beings and of the calling they exercise.

Agriculture – Catholic social teaching emphasizes the nobility of farming; the importance of careful stewardship of the land; the promotion of the family farm; popular participation to ensure that food production is not just in a few hands; a national policy of self-reliance so that primary emphasis is on producing the foods our own people need, with the surplus being geared to export; the use of appropriate technology so as to combat the notion that bigger is always better.

The Image of the Church in Catholic Social Teaching

The official documents of Catholic Social Teaching (approximately a dozen in all) begin with Pope Leo XIII's *Rerum Novarum* in 1891 and extend to Pope Benedict XVI's social encyclical of 2009. As we reflect on more than 100 years of official Catholic Social Teaching, we see a definite image of the Church emerge. (a) The Church is not just a community to give us personal peace ("Don't disturb my prayers," a private view of Church); (b) The Church is not just a community to ensure social peace. (c) The Church is a community engaged in bringing about change or conversion, not just in each person but also in everything human: society, culture, economic and political institutions. It is the "yeast of the gospel," put here to transform everything.

We should note also that every image of heaven appearing in the Bible pictures it as a community of people (a wedding banquet, a great city with its gates open on all sides), so we need to be "community-minded people" here in order to be properly disposed to become part of that eternal community.

We should get to know the rich treasury of Catholic Social Documents. They can be found on the Vatican website and on www.catholiclabor.org

For a quick "reader-friendly" course in the Church's Social Teaching, see *The Social Attitudes of a Catholic* by Michael Ryan (Solidarity Books 2005)

Conversion Includes Remaking Some of our Social Images

To be in tune with Catholic Social Teaching, we may have to undergo some "social conversion," by revising some of our long-held images of ownership; work; labour unions; people on welfare; employment insurance; etc. "Every real conversion begins on the level of our directive images; by changing his imagination, a man changes his life." (Paul Ricoeur).

Being a Catholic is more than saying our prayers and keeping out of trouble. It is also a matter of paying attention to what we are already involved in just by being part of our society and our economy. Many of our culture's social and economic practices do harm to others and lead people into performing unjust actions. For this reason, they are referred to as instances of "social sin." In response to such social sin, we have to develop the virtue of social charity (a genuine love of the common good, heartfelt concern about what kind of society and community we have) and practise social justice (joint action with others to change sinful practices and structures so that the common good will be restored and promoted).

Audiovisuals
Committed to Change (CCODP)
Is Wal-Mart Good for America? (PBS Home Video)

Chapter 14

PRAYER

Several years ago, in a pastoral letter to the people of his diocese, a bishop in the United States reflected on the importance of reaching out to Catholics who were no longer practising the faith. In the course of that letter, he asked the question: Why do people get away from practising their faith? The first reason he himself offered is provocative. He said it was because some people simply do not experience the power and presence of God when they go to Mass.

If this is true – and I think it is – there could be many causes that account for it. However, I strongly suspect that the major cause is the fact that many people lack a personal relationship with Christ. Without such a relationship, the Mass tends to become for them simply a ritual, a formality. The kind of relationship we need if we are going to be disposed to meet Jesus in the Mass and the sacraments is one that is built up especially in personal or private prayer. Hence, this topic is important.

Definition

Prayer is the raising of the mind and heart to God. Note the words, "mind" and "heart." Prayer is from the depths of our being; it is not simply something on the lips.

Kinds of Prayer

Public prayer – We think here especially of the liturgy, which is the official, public prayer of the Church. In the liturgy, it is primarily Christ who prays. He is our way to the Father. He is our mediator, whose prayer is always pleasing to the Father. We are joined to him by Baptism and so we are taken up into his prayer. When Jesus offers himself to the Father in our name at Mass, we too, along with the priest, offer him, and we offer ourselves along with him.

Then there is the Breviary, or the Liturgy of the Hours, which is the official daily prayer of the Church. Different parts of it are offered at various parts of the day, so that it becomes a way of consecrating the entire day to

God. It is the prayer offered by every Catholic priest each day, and the prayer that is offered together or "in choir" in a more solemn way by the members of many religious communities within the Church. Here it is the whole Church that prays, and because the Church is the Bride of Christ, Jesus offers the Church's prayer along with his before the throne of the Father.

When we understand what the liturgy is, we see what a powerful prayer it is. Since it is first and foremost the prayer of Jesus, it is clearly much more powerful and important than any purely personal prayer we offer.

Private Prayer – This is the kind of prayer in which one person, or a group of persons, simply pray on their own, rather than officially in the name of the Church. It would be a mistake, however, to think that this kind of prayer is not important. On the contrary, this kind of prayer is essential for us to build up our personal relationship with Christ. The fact is that the two kinds of prayer need one another. Private prayer, without involvement in the liturgy, lacks a sense of the Church, and does not possess the power of the prayer Jesus offers through his Church. Liturgical prayer, however, without a lived relationship to Christ on the part of those who offer it, tends to become impersonal, routine, boring, and uninteresting. So we need to develop a strong, personal prayer life. When we have such a prayer life, the liturgy can become a powerful experience for us.

Private Prayer

Though this prayer is offered privately by us, it can still be a prayer in which we use the words of others. Thus, our private prayer may consist in a recitation of the Our Father, the Hail Mary, and the formal Acts of Faith, Hope and Charity. In the beginning at least, and probably throughout our life, it is helpful to use some prayers we have learned by heart. These are the prayers on which we can always fall back. We should train ourselves to offer such prayers thoughtfully, and from the heart, making them our own as we pray them. The gospels show us that Jesus knew many of the psalms by heart and that he prayed those psalms. Formal prayers that were composed by other people can of course become routine and superficial. However, they are usually well thought-out and have a depth that our informal prayers may lack. They can also challenge us, where our informal prayers may be too self-centered. They are also prayers we can more easily offer with others.

Private prayer can also be informal, that is, prayer that is offered with our own words. At least with the passage of time we should find ourselves able to do this. Good spiritual reading nourishes this kind of prayer. Such reading should include Holy Scripture, and other recognized spiritual classics, as well as the writing of dependable contemporary authors.

Jesus is our Model in Prayer

The incident of Jesus remaining behind in the Temple at Jerusalem when he was twelve years old gives us a glimpse of the manner in which he lived in daily awareness of the presence of the heavenly Father. That same awareness shows up in his parables and his teaching. Throughout the Gospel, we see him praying for sustained periods, sometimes all night, at decisive moments in his ministry. The most outstanding feature of his prayer is the fact that he always prays with a great spirit of reverence for the Father. His prayer at the agony in the garden is, "Not my will, Father, but yours be done." On the cross he prays, "Father, into your hands I commend my spirit." The "Our Father" is the ideal prayer. Learning to say it slowly, reflectively and thoughtfully is an important way for us to imitate the prayer of Jesus and to grow in prayer.

Forms of Prayer

Adoration – Some of the great Greek thinkers who lived several centuries before Christ insisted that humans find their fulfillment, not in themselves, but in going beyond themselves. In particular, some of the great philosophers insisted that humans find their proper goal by reaching out to the Absolute. are the only earthly creatures that do grow and exodus, win the name of all,y, "standing out from oneself," is the origin of our English term, "ecstasy." The Latin term, *alienatio*, which gives us our English word "alienation," originally had a positive meaning; it is by getting away from ourselves, reaching out to the other, and especially to the Supreme Other, that we fulfill our humanity. This is why we are never more human than when we pray. We are the only earthly creatures that do pray, and we do so in the name of all creation. Adoration involves a vivid awareness of who God is (our creator and sustainer) and who we are (creatures).

Thanksgiving – God sustains us as the singer sustains his song. All that we are and have is gift. It is a gift that is constantly being renewed each moment that God maintains us in existence. The Mass is called the "Eucharist," a Greek word meaning "thanksgiving." We should never cease to thank God.

Sorrow for sin – This is something we need to express regularly. In particular, we should develop the habit of examining our conscience at the end of each day, to see what our response to God has been during the day. Then we should conclude that examination with a heartfelt expression of sorrow for the ways we have failed God and offended his goodness during the day. We should learn an act of contrition by heart.

Petition – Jesus tells us that if we ask, we will receive, and if we knock, the door will be opened to us. We pray both for others and for ourselves. Prayer of petition is a way of acknowledging the fact that we are in the hands of our Father, who desires only what is good for us. This does not mean that we will always receive what we ask for, since the Father sees the whole picture; we see only a tiny part of it.

Qualities of Prayer

Reverence – Our prayer needs to reflect an awareness of who God is. It is a good practice to pray on our knees, at least for a time, for then the whole person prays. It is also good to remember that, in moments when we find it hard to pray, the fact that we simply try to stay in God's presence, even if it is hard to keep our mind on God, means that our whole body prays; our very bodily presence expresses reverence.

Confidence – Of course, God hears us when we pray. There is no question about it. God is our Father.

Perseverance – Some of Jesus' parables stress the importance of this quality. It may be that only our perseverance will open us up sufficiently to God so that we are properly disposed to receive what we are asking. One of the most famous examples of this quality is St. Monica, who prayed for twenty years for the conversion of her son, Augustine. When the prayer was finally answered, it was answered in a powerful way, for Augustine became someone who is possibly the most important figure in the Church's early centuries, a great bishop and scholar.

Submission to God's Will – In all our prayer there must always be the proviso: "God willing!"

When Should We Pray?

In the morning – We should offer our day, and all we will do. This is a priestly act. It consecrates our day to God, and reminds us that, since we are offering our whole day to God this is the reason why we should try to do everything this day as perfectly as we can.

In the evening – Here is the place for a good examination of conscience.

At meals – Grace at mealtimes is a good opportunity to recall ourselves to God's presence.

When tempted – We should get into habit of praying right away when temptation first presents itself to our mind.

Short prayers throughout the day – This is an important habit to develop. There is a story of a man who asked whether it was permissible to chew gum while he was praying. He was told, "No." However, he was also told that it is permissible, even desirable, to pray while he was chewing gum. This second piece of advice concerned keeping oneself in God's presence, whatever we are doing during the day. There are many short prayers we can become accustomed to saying to ourselves, such as "My Jesus mercy."

To Whom Do We Pray?

Strictly speaking, prayer is offered to the Father, through the Son, in union with the Holy Spirit. We should never lose sight of the fact that God is the Trinity.

We can also pray, however, to Jesus and to the Holy Spirit in particular situations.

Contemplative Prayer

This term may sound forbidding, and we may feel that contemplative prayer is only for people like those living in monasteries. Yet it is really a form of prayer that every Christian should try to develop. It consists in a simple awareness of God's presence. We try to maintain an interior silence and to let our attention rest simply with God. It is sometimes described as an effort to hear God. Most writers recommend the use of a "mantra," that is, a short phrase to keep bringing us back into God's presence, something like "My Jesus mercy" or "My Lord and my God."

In the Old Testament, the young Samuel was taught to say, "Speak Lord, your servant is listening." Far too often, our prayer takes the form, "Listen Lord, your servant is speaking." Contemplative prayer reminds us to turn that around!

Prayer Requires Effort and Perseverance

There is an old story of a labourer meeting a monk riding a horse on a country road. The labourer had just put in a long day and he chided the monk about what an easy life he had, with nothing to do but pray. The monk replied that prayer was more difficult than the labourer realized. To illustrate this, the monk offered to give the man his horse if he could say the entire Our Father without any distractions. The man said that was easy. He started off, "Our Father, who art in heaven," but then stopped and asked, "Will you give me the saddle too?" The story makes it clear that all of us need to work at prayer.

We must have a will to pray. We must learn to pray. It does not just happen. It is not as simple as breathing, though it is as necessary to our spiritual life as breathing is to our physical life. It involves building up a personal love and friendship with Christ. This is essential in our Christian life.

It is helpful to have a regular time each day that we set aside for prayer, time we spend in God's presence. We have to battle to stay with it. We must be prepared even to spend an extended time in prayer. We need to be convinced that this is the best use of our time; we are not wasting time when we prolong our prayer.

The Words of St. Alphonsus Liguori

This great 18th century moral theologian, who is honoured as a Doctor of the Church (one whose teaching the Church sees as especially apt for our guidance) states: "Those who pray are certainly saved; those who do not pray are certainly damned." It is hard to find a more convincing reason for prayer than this!

The Place for Prayer

Where should we pray? Of course, we can pray anywhere. However, there are two especially favoured places we should keep in mind. First, we should use whatever opportunities we have to pray before the Blessed Sacrament. This is truly a privileged place to pray. Second, if possible, it is good to set aside a prayer space at home, a private spot of our own where we can be alone, and a place that contains objects, perhaps a crucifix, sacred pictures, a Bible, that will help us to pray.

Video

What Catholics Believe About Prayer (Liguori)

Chapter 15

DEVOTIONAL LIFE, VENERATION OF MARY AND THE SAINTS

The Communion of Saints

There is a clause in the Apostles Creed in which we affirm our belief in "the communion of saints." What does this mean? *Acts* 4:32 says the early Christians "had everything in common." Because they had a great sense of how our Baptism makes us one body, one family, one community, they even shared their earthly goods as a sign of the spiritual goods they had in common. The word "communion" means a sharing of family life, and a sharing of spiritual goods. The Creed, written a century or so later, reflects the awareness that this oneness we have and this sharing of spiritual goods extend beyond this life. We continue to form one family, and to share spiritual goods, not only with our fellow Christians on earth, but also with those in heaven, and, as we shall see in another session, with those in purgatory.

"Saints" means those joined to the Holy One, Jesus, and therefore those called to be saints. St. Paul writes his letters to the "saints." For example, we read, "To all the saints in Christ Jesus who are in Philippi" (*Philippians* 1:1).

We might think of this sharing of spiritual goods among the "saints" as having a common bank account, into which all of us make deposits, and from which all of us can make withdrawals. Obviously, the major depositor is Jesus. However, our prayers, our penances, and sufferings patiently borne can be deposits as well. St. Paul writes: "I am now rejoicing in my sufferings for your sake, and in my flesh I am completing what is lacking in Christ's afflictions for the sake of his body, that is, the church" (*Colossians* 1:24).

Another image that helps here is to think of ourselves as one great support group for one other. The daily awareness that we live in the company of the saints is a real sign of genuine Christian faith. The saints truly are with us in our daily life.

The Saints as People Who Pray for Us

St. Paul asked his fellow Christians to pray for him: "I appeal to you, brothers and sisters, by our Lord Jesus Christ and by the love of the Spirit, to join me in earnest prayer to God on my behalf, that I may be rescued from the unbelievers in Judea, and that my ministry to Jerusalem may be acceptable to the saints, so that by God's will I may come to you with joy and be refreshed in your company" (*Romans* 15:30-32). "At the same time pray for us as well that God will open to us a door for the word" (*Colossians* 4:3). *"Beloved, pray for us"* (*I Thessalonians* 5:25). If it is proper to ask our friends to pray for us while they are alive, how much more proper it is to ask them to pray for us when they are with God in heaven. St. Dominic, when dying, said, "Do not weep, for I shall be more useful to you after my death and I shall help you more effectively than during my life." St. Thérèse of Lisieux said: "I want to spend my heaven doing good upon earth."

The Saints as Good Examples

We do not "worship" the saints or Mary, the greatest of them. We venerate or honour them. They are our heroes, and great heroes at that! The saints are wonderful examples to us, and few things can inspire us to live the Christian life as much as reading good lives of the saints. Here are people who lived as we do, and faced what we have to face, yet who followed Jesus in truly heroic fashion. The practice of taking a saint's name at baptism gives one a patron saint to study and imitate.

One of the greatest features of Catholic life is the calendar of the saints. It includes men and women, old and young, rich and poor, nobles and slaves, those dedicated to celibacy and those committed in the married state. We find remarkable saints in every part of the world, and in every age, including our own. Many people have been drawn into the Church by the example of the saints. Reading such documents as St. Therese of Lisieux's *The Story of a Soul,* or the diaries of Dorothy Day (who is presently being officially considered for sainthood), can be a transforming experience. These Christian heroes are a forceful reminder to us that Jesus calls his followers to become saints, not "celebrities."

Who are the saints? Early saints are people who were popularly recognized as such by the general body of Christians. By the year 1200, however, the Church introduced the canonization process for recognizing people as saints. It is a long, careful examination of a person's life and writings, and must be supported by several miracles obtained through asking this person's intercession. The three stages on the road to canonization are: venerable, blessed, saint.

Mary, the Greatest of the Saints

Mary, the Mother of God – We honour Mary because of her unique role in God's Plan of Salvation. Just as we honour public officials who did great work for the common good, so we honour this person who was so important to God's Plan. Just as we honour the mother of our friend, so we honour the woman who is mother of our Lord. See how the New Testament honours her: "Greetings favoured one! The Lord is with you!" (*Luke* 1:28) and again, "Surely, from now on all generations will call me blessed" (*Luke* 1:48).

Mary, The Ideal Disciple – Above all, the New Testament presents Mary as the model of discipleship. This is most apparent in St. Luke's Gospel. She was one of those who "hear the word of God and do it" (8:21). "Mary treasured all these words and pondered them in her heart" (*Luke* 2:19)

Consider the significance of the following. First, Mary's response to the angel at the Annunciation: "Here am I, the servant of the Lord, let it be with me according to your word" (*Luke* 1:38). Second, the greeting by Elizabeth at the Visitation, "Blessed are you among women, and blessed is the fruit of your womb. And why has this happened to me, that the mother of my Lord comes to me" (*Luke* 1: 42-43). Third, Mary's words at Cana: "Do whatever he tells you" (*John* 2:5). Fourth, the scene on Calvary: "Standing near the cross of Jesus were his mother, and his mother's sister, Mary the wife of Clopas, and Mary Magdalene. When Jesus saw his mother and the disciple whom he loved standing beside her, he said to his mother 'Woman, here is your son'. Then he said to the disciple, 'Here is your mother'" (*John* 19: 25-27).

Mary the Safeguard of the Truth about Jesus. "They saw the child with Mary his mother" (*Matthew* 2:11). It is always with Mary that we find Jesus. Every time we look at her, she points us to her son. The Council of Ephesus in 431 applied the title *Theotokos*, that is, "Mother of God," to Mary, thereby reaffirming the Church's faith in Jesus as truly God. There is a famous story about a man who dropped into a Catholic Church one day and heard the priest, in his sermon, say that "Mary is the Mother of God." The expression bothered him for years. How could any creature possibly be the mother of God? Finally, he came to terms with the truth of the incarnation, and realized what it really means, that Jesus actually is God! Devotion to Mary has historically served to keep people from seeing Jesus as only a man. "Mother of God" makes us focus on one Person, two Natures. Jesus is God the Son, who possesses both the divine nature and a true human nature taken from the mother who bore him.

It is in this light also that we need to see two of the truths about Mary that have been officially defined by the Catholic Church. In 1854, the Church defined the doctrine of the Immaculate Conception, that is, the teaching that Mary was preserved from the taint of original sin from the moment when she was conceived in the womb of her mother, St. Anne. In 1950, the Church defined the teaching that is really a corollary to this one, that Mary, being free from original sin, was also free from bodily corruption, the sign of sin, and that she was taken bodily into heaven at the end of her life. Note that no place is, or ever has been honoured as the site of Mary's burial, though the tombs of Peter and Paul, for example, were important to Christians at an early date.

Protestants often find these two doctrines difficult to accept, since they seem to make too much of Mary, and to distract us from Christ. In reality, the effect of these two doctrines is the opposite; they serve to shine a brighter light on the truth of the incarnation. Behind these two teachings about Mary lie centuries of Christian reflection on who Jesus is. Since Jesus is really and truly God the Son who has taken on a true human nature, and since his coming marked the victory over the sin of Adam, we can see how important it is that the woman from whom he took his humanity should herself have been preserved, in view of the death her Son was going to endure, from the least contact with sin, and should also be the first one, after him, to be glorified body and soul in heaven.

Honouring Mary means taking with total seriousness the truth about who her son is. Consider these words of St. Ephraim the Syrian, who died in 373

A.D.: "Thou alone, O Jesus, with thy Mother are beautiful in every way; for there is no blemish in thee, my Lord, and no stain in thy Mother." The New Testament itself testifies to Mary's holiness and it appears to connect this with the fact that she was chosen to be the mother of Jesus. Scripture makes it clear that God demands holiness in those who approach him. In addition to the ways in which Mary's holiness is proclaimed in the infancy Gospel, the fact that God took special steps to preserve her virginity suggests that God granted her special holiness in view of the Child she was going to bear. Moreover her role as the "new Eve" (cf. *Genesis* 3:15) appears to call for one who was preserved in a state of sinlessness from the time of her conception.

The Hail Mary – The first part of this prayer is from the New Testament scenes of the Annunciation and the Visitation. The second part, which asks Mary to pray for us sinners, "now and at the hour of our death" recalls St. John's statement that Mary stood at the foot of Jesus' cross while he died.

The Rosary – The mechanics of saying it are easily explained. The devotion itself originated probably in the 12th century, and arose from two main causes: the growth in a personal devotion to Jesus and to Mary, and the desire of people to have a closer participation in the official prayer of the Church (the Breviary or the Divine Office). The heart of the Divine Office is the 150 psalms. Consequently, many people got into the habit of saying 150 Our Fathers as "the poor man's breviary." These were divided in various ways, and eventually into groups of ten (or decades). Strings of beads were used to count these prayers (cf. Moslem practice of doing the same thing).

Devotion to Mary followed a similar course. Eventually the modern form of 5 decades, each beginning with an Our Father, including 10 Hail Marys, and concluding with a Glory be to the Father, took shape as a Marian devotion. The Rosary is meant to be a way of meditating on the great truths of our faith, as we recite the prayers, using our beads to keep track of them. Traditionally, these were called the Mysteries of the Rosary. For centuries, there were five Joyful, five Sorrowful, and five Glorious mysteries. Pope John Paul II added five more mysteries, called the "Luminous Mysteries." By the 15th century, the Rosary as we know it today had largely taken shape. The Rosary continues to be popular among Catholics, and is in many ways a very comforting prayer, as well as being one to which it is easy to turn, e.g. when travelling. Carrying one's Rosary wherever one goes is also a wonderful external sign of devotion to Mary, the mother of God.

Video

What Catholics Believe about Mary and the Saints (Liguori)

Chapter 16

THE CHURCH IN DAILY LIFE

Since the Church is the presence among us of the Risen Christ we are assured that it will faithfully, and without error, teach us the truths he entrusted to it for our salvation. This is what we mean by the infallibility of the Church. That infallibility is a feature of the official teaching of the Church under certain well-defined conditions. For example, when the pope and the bishops gather for an Ecumenical or General Council of the Church they may state that they are defining some particular truth as a matter of Catholic faith, and therefore as something to be believed by all Catholics. The Second Vatican Council in 1962 to 1965 stated that it did not intend to define any doctrines officially. In contrast, the Council of Trent in 1545 to 1563 solemnly defined several doctrines that had been denied by the Protestant reformers.

The pope alone may also solemnly define a doctrine under the following four conditions: he must speak as a public person in relation to the whole Church; he must intend to define a doctrine and actually do so; he must speak on a matter of "faith or morals," and he must intend to bind the whole Church. The last pope to act in this manner was Pius XII, when he defined the Assumption of the Blessed Virgin into heaven in 1950.

Infallibility should not be confused with revelation. It does not involve revealing some new doctrine but rather solemnly declaring something already entrusted, either explicitly or implicitly, to the apostles by the Lord. Nor is it a form of inspiration. It is, instead, a form of divine assistance, preserving the Church from error in what it solemnly teaches us as a matter of faith. This does not preclude the possibility that the Church, at some later date, may be able to state that doctrine even more fully and clearly for us.

Much of the guidance the Church gives us in daily life does not involve an exercise of infallibility but is rather the Church teaching us like a good mother. Such teaching should be accepted in a spirit of faith and confidence in the guidance of the Holy Spirit. We will now consider three of the ways in which the Church teaches us in daily life: through the liturgical year, through the use of the sacramentals, and through the precepts of the Church.

1. THE LITURGICAL YEAR

For historical reasons, the civil and liturgical calendars are different. As we all know, the civil calendar begins each year on January 1st. The liturgical calendar, however, starts on the First Sunday of Advent, which occurs somewhere around the end of November or the beginning of December, depending on the year.

What we call "the liturgical year" is the annual "re-living" by the Church of the life of Christ, by celebrating, on appropriate dates, the mysteries of his life, death, and resurrection. Within the liturgical year, we observe particular seasons, such as Advent, Christmas, Lent, Easter, and Ordinary Time. The scriptural readings used in the liturgy always reflect the particular season.

Catholics in some of the Eastern Rites of the Catholic Church observe Christmas and Easter on different dates than those observed by Catholics of the Latin Rite.

The Liturgical Seasons

Advent – This four-week season recalls the long period before the first coming of Christ. It also looks forward to his Second Coming at the end of the world, and of course to our sacramental re-living of his first coming in our Christmas celebration. The Old Testament readings recall our fallen human condition and our need of the Redeemer. They also give us the words of the various prophets who look forward to the coming of the Messiah, and so arouse in us a sense of longing.

Christmas – This feast concentrates on the infancy Gospels of Matthew and Luke, and reflects on the great mystery of the incarnation.

Epiphany – This occasion, part of the Christmas season, recalls the story of the Magi, and celebrates the calling of the Gentiles to the faith.

Lent – This season, which begins on Ash Wednesday, and lasts for 40 days, has several purposes. (1) It is the proximate preparation for Baptism or Reception into Full Communion with the Catholic Church, at the Easter Vigil, of those who have been going through the R.C.I.A. program. (2) It is a period of preparation for those already baptized so that they will be disposed for the renewal of their Baptismal promises that takes place in the liturgy of the Easter Vigil and Easter Sunday. (3) It is a period of public prayer and penance, a time of personal renewal for all Christians, as we make ready to celebrate the great events of the passion, death, and resurrection of Jesus during Holy Week.

Holy Week – This week begins with the Palm Sunday triumphal entry of Jesus into Jerusalem when people greeted him with palm branches. For us it is a time of reaffirming our loyalty to Christ as our King, the King who will give his life for us during this week. Holy Thursday, when we have the Mass of the Last Supper, is a celebration of the gifts of the Holy Eucharist and the priesthood. Good Friday, when we solemnly read the account of Jesus' passion and death, is the only day in the year when we do not celebrate Mass. Instead, we have a Scripture and prayer service followed by Communion with the Sacred Hosts consecrated at the Holy Thursday Mass. On Holy Saturday evening, we observe the great Easter Vigil. It begins with a Light Service, which includes the blessing of the Easter Candle that represents the Risen Lord. This is followed by a Service of Readings from the Old Testament, which prepares us for Baptism. Then we begin the Mass of the Resurrection, during which we bless the Baptismal water, and then receive into the Church those who have been preparing for this in the recent months. All other Catholics renew their Baptismal promises at this time.

Easter – This entire season celebrates the triumph of Jesus over sin and death, and reflects on its meaning for our lives. At the end of this season, we celebrate the Ascension of Jesus into heaven.

Pentecost – This Sunday celebrates the descent of the Holy Spirit on the infant church, and is rightly called the birthday of the Church.

Ordinary Time – The Sundays of Ordinary Time take us through the public life of Jesus. On weekdays, the Church also celebrates some feasts of the saints, to put before us examples of the Christian life and encourage us.

The Scripture Readings

The Constitution on the Sacred Liturgy of Vatican II states: "The treasures of the Bible are to be opened up more lavishly, so that richer fare may be provided for the faithful at the table of God's Word. In this way a more representative portion of the holy Scriptures will be read to the people over a set cycle of years" (no. 51).

The Sunday Gospels during Ordinary Time follow a three-year cycle. Year A is the year of Matthew, Year B the year of Mark and year C the year of Luke. John's Gospel is featured at other liturgical times, e.g. during Lent and Easter. The first reading is usually a passage from an Old Testament book that fits in with the theme of the Gospel reading for that Sunday. The second reading takes us through other New Testament books whose theme fits in with the particular liturgical season.

Today Anglicans, Lutherans and several other Protestant Churches follow a Sunday Lectionary that is like the one used by Catholics.

2. THE SACRAMENTALS

Jesus gave us the seven sacraments. The sacraments are actions of Christ, and so in them we meet Christ. Because the Risen Lord lives in the Church, it is really he who meets us through the official actions of the Church. This is an important consideration. No matter who the priest that administers the sacrament, that sacrament has its effect unless we put an obstacle in its way (such as an intention not to receive the sacrament).

Distinct from the sacraments are what we call sacramentals. These are sacred signs that bear a resemblance to the sacraments. However, they are given to us by the Church. They were not instituted by Christ but by the Church. They are special blessings or blessed objects that the Church uses (a) to inspire our devotion, and (b) to seek God's help for us. The sacramentals gain their power from the fact that the prayer they involve is the prayer of the Church. It is not just a private prayer. This is important, because Jesus always hears the prayer of his bride, the Church.

Sacramentals always involve a prayer, which is accompanied by a specific sign, such as laying on of hands, sign of the cross, sprinkling with holy water.

Sacramentals include:
• Blessings of persons
• Blessings of things

• Blessed objects

Certain blessings have a lasting importance because they (1) consecrate persons to God, or (2) reserve objects and places for liturgical use.

Among lasting blessings intended for persons are the blessing of an Abbot or Abbess of a monastery, the consecration of virgins, the rite of religious profession, and the blessings of certain ministries of the Church, such as Eucharistic Ministers and Lectors.

Among lasting blessings intended for things are the dedication or blessing of a church, altar, chalice, holy oils, vestments, bells, etc.

Some sacramentals can be conferred only by an ordained person, but many can also be given by lay people (who thus express their sharing in the common priesthood of Christ by reason of their baptism). Thus, parents can bless their children.

Sacramentals are not magic. They depend on the faith and devotion of the persons concerned, even though they derive their power from the prayer of the Church.

Sacramental objects, such as blessed medals and blessed crucifixes are reminders for us.

3. THE PRECEPTS OF THE CHURCH

One of the official books of the Church is the Code of Canon Law. It contains 1752 canons or laws that govern the life of the Church. A small number of them affect all of us, and these have come to be referred to as the Precepts of the Church. Most people list six of them.

First Precept: to keep holy Sundays and Holydays of Obligation. We have already spoken of the requirement to participate in Mass on Sundays. Holydays of Obligation are major feasts when we have the same obligation to assist at Mass as we have on Sunday. The number of such days varies from one country to the next and we are always supposed to follow the rule of the country in which we find ourselves. In Canada there are only two such Holydays: Christmas (December 25th) and the Feast of Mary the Mother of God (New Year's Day, January 1st).

Second Precept: to receive the Holy Eucharist at least once a year, during the Easter Season. This is the so-called "Easter Duty" to which older Catholics sometimes refer. It specifies a minimum. If we think of how difficult it is to raise a family on the legal minimum wage, we can see how hard it is to live the Christian life if we try to get by with this minimum reception of the Eucharist. Our goal should be to receive the Eucharist every time we assist at Mass, so long as we are free from serious sin and properly disposed.

Third Precept: to confess our sins at least once a year. Again this is a minimum (which, strictly speaking, obliges us only if we are guilty of mortal sin). Here too, the effort to live the Christian life without receiving the Sacrament of Reconciliation on a regular basis means depriving ourselves of one of the greatest helps Jesus gave us to live as his disciples. We should receive this sacrament regularly, at least several times a year.

Fourth Precept: to fast and abstain on the days appointed. The Church is here requiring of us a minimum form of penance in order to remind us of our basic Christian obligation to do penance. We need to do penance in order to acknowledge our sins and the excesses in our life, in order to make some sort of personal reparation for them, and in order to practice some form of self-denial that will train us to fight temptation and so to stay faithful. The advantage of this Church-prescribed form of penance is that it is something social, something we do together as Catholics, and therefore a way in which we express solidarity with one another, and support one another.

Fasting, strictly speaking, means eating only one full meal a day. Something may be taken at the other two meals, but those two together must not equal another full meal. Of course, there is to be no eating between meals. Some people may be able to observe a stricter fast; others may not be able to observe the usual fast, but may adopt some modified form. The important thing is to act generously and with a good motive. Fasting obliges people from the age of 18 until the age of 59. In Canada at present, there are only two compulsory fast days: Ash Wednesday and Good Friday.

Abstinence means refraining from meat or meat products (soup made from meat, etc.). Abstinence obliges everyone 14 years of age and older. In Canada, Ash Wednesday and Good Friday are days of abstinence. Normally all Fridays are to be observed as days of abstinence, and especially the Fridays of Lent. This is a time-honoured way of recognizing Friday as the day on which Jesus died on the cross for us. Friday should always be a special day, a penitential day, for a Christian. If, for some good reason, a person is unable to observe a Friday as a day of abstinence they may substitute some other form of penance, or some good work like visiting the sick, assisting at Mass, giving alms or saying the rosary.

Fifth Precept: to observe the laws of the Church concerning marriage. We have already spoken about this in our treatment of the Sacrament of Matrimony.

Sixth Precept: to contribute to the support of the Church. This support should be for our local church and for the Church worldwide; this is part of what it means to say that all of us must be missionaries. Such support is also a way of giving back to God a portion of what God has given to us. In the Mosaic Law, the Israelites were required to give a tithe, that is, one-tenth of their harvest or income to God by donating it to the Temple. However, in that society, the Temple used a portion of that to support widows, orphans and others in need. In our society many of those functions are carried out by our government, using money we contribute through our taxes. Our own contribution to the Church should be determined by us personally, considering such things as how good God has been to us, what the needs of our family are, and what the particular needs of our parish are.

Video

God in the Dock (Paulist Productions)

This half-hour video is based on one of C.S. Lewis' books and reflects on the mystery of suffering. It is a Hollywood-produced drama, made with seasoned actors. Those people who are going through an R.C.I.A. program find themselves, at this point, in the season of Lent. This season directs our attention to the suffering of Jesus for us, and so it is an appropriate time to consider the mystery of suffering. In conjunction with this video, readers might want to look at Chapter 2 of my book, *In the Light of Faith*, Second Edition (Solidarity Books 2008), "Faith and the mystery of evil."

Chapter 17

THE LAST THINGS

Life as a Journey

For the French Existentialist philosopher, Jean-Paul Sartre, who was an atheist, the human person is "une passion inutile," a meaningless bundle of activity. In contrast, Gabriel Marcel, a convert to the Catholic Church, and also an important figure in the Existentialist Movement, sees the human person as "homo viator"(a pilgrim).

We are pilgrims, people on a journey. All of us have a sense of responsibility for ourselves; we are aware that we are somehow answerable for our lives, and must expect to give an accounting at some future point. In fact, all human activity presupposes some sense of a goal in life; we would not undertake any actions unless we were in pursuit of some sort of goal for our life. So life is properly seen as a journey.

Three Senses of This Journey

Human History as a Journey – Whereas some ancient cultures saw history as cyclical, as something that simply repeats itself over and over again, the Bible sees history as moving toward a goal. A modern secular ideology, Marxist Communism, similarly views history as moving toward a goal, the "classless society." This strong sense of a goal was borrowed by Marx, both from the philosopher G.W.F. Hegel, who was influenced by Christian thought, and from his own Jewish roots in the prophets. One of the strongest expressions of history moving toward a goal in the New Testament is found in the *Book of Revelation*. The book is addressed to Christians facing persecution, and it reminds us that God is the Lord of history, with the result that the ultimate victory is God's. (*Revelation* is a misunderstood book. It does not predict the future. Its violent language and colourful images are meant to force us to make a choice for Christ every day. Moreover, it points out that the whole world will participate in God's final victory. This world will be transformed, not destroyed.)

The Church as a People on a Journey – This theme was much

emphasized in the documents of Vatican II. As people on a journey, we belong to the age of imperfect fulfillment. Thus, the Old Testament is full of images that look forward to fulfillment when the Messiah comes. The New Testament is the age of fulfillment, but only partial fulfillment. It in turn looks forward to the end of time when we will have complete fulfillment. For example, the manna in the Old Testament was a sign of the Blessed Eucharist, which in turn is a sign of the beatific vision. In each case, the Old Testament image simply represents a future reality; the New Testament sacrament is that reality, but still in an imperfect or veiled state. We look forward to the complete reality. The sacraments, in this sense, are imperfect; the Church, the fundamental sacrament, is imperfect; the union we already have with Christ is imperfect.

Each Person is Someone on a Journey – We will not understand Christianity unless we see it as involving a looking forward to eternal life with Christ. That life in Christ begins here with baptism (our life of sanctifying grace, by which we are raised to the level of a child of God), but it involves all the hardships of the journey here (like people on a wagon train), and will be fulfilled at the end of time when Christ comes again. We cannot see the point of faithfulness and commitment in this world, nor of sacrifice and renunciation for the sake of the Kingdom, without this belief in eternal life.

Death

For the Christian, the word "death" has a new meaning. What death really involves is the ultimate loss of control. In *Genesis* 3, the sin committed was one of wanting total control: "You will be like gods, knowing good and evil," was the promise made to Adam and Eve by the serpent. Overcoming this sort of pride in ourselves is a matter of admitting that we are not in control. To accept the ways in which we are not in control is what the New Testament calls "dying to self." This is a greater reality for all of us as we get older, yet it is also real for younger people, because many things are beyond the control of all of us. To accept this fact with a love of God's Providence is to die to self. (Note that this is not a call to passivity). Our model is Jesus, especially in his passion and death. Consider especially the attitude taken by Jesus during his agony in the garden: "Not my will, Father, but yours be done." When there is complete death to self, then life in Christ can really take over in us. Once this death has occurred in us, physical death is readily accepted.

What Comes after Death?

The domain of theology dealing with death and what occurs after death is called eschatology, which means the study of the last things. The language we use in discussing what happens after death is not a language of description. How can we describe what we have never experienced and cannot even imagine? Rather, it is a collection of images and pictures that (a) say something about what our relationship will be to God and to others in the next life; and (b) represent much more an expression of hope than of knowledge. (This hope is rooted, however, in our faith).

Judgment – In the presence of the Supreme Truth, all our "masks" will fall away. We will see clearly the complete truth of our own situation before God. We speak of particular judgment that takes place at our own death and of the general judgment that will take place at the end of the world.

Eternal Life – This means total union with Jesus Christ, and through him, with the Father and the Holy Spirit. Since God is the source of being and life, this will be for us an experience of being totally alive. To appreciate this idea, it helps to remember that our greatest happiness in life comes from our relationships. Think of the most exciting relationship we could have with the most exciting person possible. This perhaps gives us a slight suggestion of what it will mean to have a total relationship with the Trinity. Moreover, eternal life is a social life, one lived with others. It is participation in a community gathered around Christ. Every Mass is a sort of preview of this. The New Testament speaks of eternal life as a heavenly banquet, and as a heavenly city.

The eternal life to which we look forward begins here with the life of sanctifying grace. There are many signs among us of the present reality of this life. Religious Communities that live under the vows of poverty, chastity, and obedience (new ways of relating to God, to others and to earthly goods) are signs of this heavenly city already present among us. So too are Christian married couples living in a spirit of loving and forgiving faithfulness, and the priest, joyfully embracing celibacy for the sake of the Kingdom of Heaven. In all these cases, we see the beginning of the kind of relationships we hope to enjoy forever. When we reflect on all this, it suggests to us that we should occasionally ask ourselves, "Am I living in the world of faith or in the purely secular world?"

Purgatory – This doctrine is a good example of something known primarily from Tradition, though there are Biblical indications, such as *II Maccabees* 12:39-45*; I Corinthians,* 3:10-15*; Matthew 5:25-26.* The constant practice of the early church and the witness of many early Christian writers, support the teaching about purgatory.

This teaching is really a matter of taking conversion seriously. Until everything about us is "turned" (converted) toward Christ, we are not capable of entering the presence of the Risen Christ. Moreover, this transformation has to operate in a free subject, and so purgatory is a process of undergoing final conversion. Our prayers can help this process. Prayers for the dead, which go back to a couple of hundred years before Christ, would make no sense without something like purgatory; people in heaven don't need our prayers and people in hell can't be helped by them. Purgatory is a wonderfully consoling teaching. It also reflects our belief in the "communion of saints." When we pray for those in purgatory, we also accept the fact that our own sins and failings helped to create the world in which our brothers and sisters in purgatory lived, and so we share responsibility for their present condition.

The Resurrection of the Body – After death, the soul survives. This is an imperfect situation; hence the Creed's reference to the resurrection of the body at the end of time. This means a body transformed and glorified like that of the risen Christ, a true body, our own body, yet changed and glorified. We could spend time speculating on how this is to come about, and there is lots of literature on it, but the most helpful thing is simply to read the New Testament accounts of the appearances of the risen Lord.

Hell – The New Testament holds the prospect of hell before us a genuine possibility, so that we will understand the seriousness and the dignity of human freedom. Our choice is the choice between life and death. Hell means the deprivation of the vision of God forever, along with the awareness that it has been our own doing. It is a state of total despair. Hell is not a punishment meted out by God. Rather if we reject God and die in that state, then we live eternally in the state we chose in life. Hell is also a state of alienation from other people, a state of total isolation. The person in hell is totally self-enclosed. (Here is a warning against becoming self-centered here). Statements about hell are not descriptions but warnings. Who is in hell? Only God knows this.

Video
    What Catholics Believe About Death and the Afterlife (Liguori)

Chapter 18

THE SACRAMENT OF CONFIRMATION AND FINAL REVIEW

1. THE SACRAMENT OF CONFIRMATION

As indicated earlier, consideration of this sacrament has been delayed until now for the benefit of those people who may be using this text as a resource in an R.C.I.A. program. Candidates for reception into the Catholic Church at the Easter Vigil, whether through baptism or through profession of faith, will all be receiving the Sacrament of Confirmation. It is important that they appreciate the significance of this great sacrament.

Baptism, Confirmation, and Eucharist constitute the "sacraments of Christian initiation." Together, they bring us into the fullness of the Christian life. Confirmation, the sacrament of Christian *maturity*, binds us more completely to the Church, gives us special strength from the Holy Spirit, and summons us to be truly zealous in spreading and defending the faith by word and deed.

In the Old Testament, the prophets said that the Spirit of the Lord would rest on the promised Messiah. We see the Spirit descend on Jesus at his baptism. Jesus then promised to send the Holy Spirit on his followers after his death and resurrection, and He did this at Pentecost. Filled with the Holy Spirit, Jesus' disciples then went out and preached boldly the Good News. From that time on, the apostles imparted to the newly baptized the gift of the Holy Spirit, by the laying on of hands. See *Acts* 8:15-17; 19:5-6; *Hebrews* 6:2.

Very early on, in order to signify better the gift of the Holy Spirit, an anointing with perfumed oil, called chrism, was added to the laying on of hands. Anointing is a sign of joy, of cleansing, of limbering up (as with athletes), of healing, and of beauty and strength. Note the name of this oil, "sacred chrism;" the word is obviously related to "Christ." There are three sacraments that join us to Christ in a special way, and each of them involves an anointing with sacred chrism: Baptism, which makes us adopted brothers

152

and sisters of Christ; Confirmation, which makes us official witnesses to Christ; and Holy Orders, which makes a person one who shares in the leadership of Christ.

By this anointing, the person is "sealed." The word looks back to the ancient practice of "sealing" a soldier, or of "branding" a slave. It shows that we belong in a special way to God. The oil of chrism, used at Confirmation, is consecrated by the bishop each year during Holy Week, and it is this chrism that is used for every Confirmation in every parish of the diocese throughout the year.

In the Eastern Rites, Confirmation is conferred immediately after Baptism. In the Latin Rite, it is conferred sometime after a person has reached the age of reason. At present, there is considerable discussion in the Latin Rite about what is the proper age for Confirmation. A strong case can be made that it should be prior to the reception of First Communion.

Preferably, it is conferred by the bishop, who officially "confirms" this person as a member of the Christian community. It signifies the person's union with the whole Church, and the person's mandate from the bishop to preach and defend the faith. It can, however, in certain circumstances, be done by a priest, for example, by the priest who receives a person into full communion with the Catholic Church, usually at the Easter Vigil. In this case, however, the priest is acting in the bishop's name and as his representative.

In conferring this sacrament, the bishop first extends his hands over those to be Confirmed, and calls down the Holy Spirit on them. Then the sacrament is conferred through the anointing on the forehead with sacred chrism, which is done by the laying on of the hand, and the words: "Be sealed with the Gift of the Holy Spirit." The sign of peace, which concludes the rite of the sacrament, signifies union in the church with the bishop and all the faithful.

Like Baptism, Confirmation can be received only once, for it marks us forever as a "Soldier of Christ." It gives the person a public status in the Church.

153

2. FINAL REVIEW

Religion – There is a true story of a priest who had spent many months instructing a man in the Catholic faith. At the end of that time, the man said to the priest, "I understand all the things you have told me, and I have no trouble accepting any of them. However I don't think I'm ready to take on the obligations of religion." The priest quite rightly replied, "You don't take on the obligations of religion. You already have them!" As the word, "religion" indicates, we are "tied to" God (Latin, *religare*) whether we acknowledge this or not. The various natural religions we see in our world and throughout history are testimony to the fact that most people have seen, and do see, that we are answerable to God for our lives.

Revealed Religion – Here we have God speaking to us. The Old Testament gives us the remarkable story of God's dealings with Abraham and the Hebrew people who sprang from him. God's plan was that this people should be a light to all the nations of the earth. To this end, God took special care of them, teaching and guiding them. Yet they failed repeatedly in the mission God had given them. Consequently, the prophets began to speak of God's promise to send an "Anointed One" ("Messiah" in Hebrew, "Christ" in Greek) who would fulfill the destiny of the people. Christians believe that Jesus is this anointed one.

Who is Jesus? – (a) The Messiah. (b) God the Son, who took on our human nature. This is surely the most startling fact of human history. Coming to terms with it involves reflecting on the doctrines of the Blessed Trinity and the Incarnation. (c) The Redeemer. Our disobedience and alienation from God as a race are overcome by Jesus' perfect obedience.

Jesus Present Among Us through His Church, His People – We have seen the various steps involved: (a) Jesus' training of his twelve apostles for a role of leadership. (b) His command to them to wait in Jerusalem after his resurrection and ascension until they were empowered. (c) His sending of the Holy Spirit on the Church-community at Pentecost. (d) The Spirit joins the Church to the Risen Christ. Jesus is the Head and the Church is his Body through which he is present and active in the world. We meet Jesus in and through the Church-community. (e) The official teaching of the Church is the teaching of Jesus, and so is infallible in guiding us. (f) The official actions of the Church (the sacraments) are the actions of Jesus and so they unfailingly have their effect.

Who are the Church? – (a) Those joined to Christ by baptism. (b) Full communion with the Church requires also accepting all that Jesus teaches us through the Church, and accepting the authority that he established: Peter (the pope) and the apostles (the bishops).

The Seven Sacraments – are as follows:

Baptism. This is fundamental. It joins us to Jesus as his brothers and sisters (and so also to his Church-community)

Confirmation. This brings us adult responsibility in the Church. It calls us to be witnesses.

The Blessed Eucharist. This is the heart of the Christian life. It is the real presence of Jesus among us under the form of food. He offers himself in our name in the Mass, which is therefore the perfect prayer.

We may receive the Eucharist in the hand or on the tongue. We may also receive both under the appearances of bread and wine or only under the appearances of bread. What is important is that we receive with faith and reverence. The word "Amen" with which we respond to the Eucharistic Minister saying "The Body of Christ" or "The Blood of Christ" is our act of faith. We should say this thoughtfully and prayerfully because it truly opens us to the Lord who comes to us.

Reconciliation. This sacrament of forgiveness restores and strengthens our union with Christ and his Church-community.

Sacrament of the Sick. Here the seriously ill meet Christ the physician.

Matrimony and *Holy Orders* – the social sacraments.

Living the Christian Life – (a) Realize your dignity and live accordingly. You have been made a son or daughter of the Father. (b) This is a call to love God with your whole heart and soul and to love your neighbour as you love yourself. Such love is an ideal toward which we are constantly reaching with God's grace. (c) Become all that you were created to be. Live in accord with the deeply human inclinations to goodness and truth that the wise God has planted in us. (d) Such a life involves the development of the virtues and brings us human flourishing. It will find its fullness however only in actual union with God face-to-face in heaven. (e) This life also means being open to the guidance of the Holy Spirit.

Clearly, living the Christian life is matter of becoming, with God's grace, a particular kind of person. It includes, but is not reducible to, observing the Ten Commandments.

Prayer – Daily communion with God is essential to living as a Christian.

Union with the Entire Family of God – (a) The Church-community on earth; (b) the saints in heaven; (c) those in purgatory. The person of faith is conscious in daily life of being part of this great community. The saints, in particular, are part of the world of faith.

Conversion – This is the work of a lifetime. It needs to be taken with total seriousness. We face heaven, hell, or purgatory. God is serious in giving us human freedom and respects our use of it.

Video

What Catholics believe about Confirmation (Liguori)

The Journey Ahead

Sometimes we hear people use expressions like "the institutional Church" or "the official Church," even "the hierarchical Church." The implication is that, distinct from each of these is something we would identify as "the real Church." This is a serious theological error. The Church is not some ideal, distinct from the "institution" or the "official organization." There is only one Church here on earth, something that is at once a visible organization and the Body of Christ. It is not some ideal, but is rather a sacrament.

As explained above, sacraments belong to our particular stage in salvation history, a stage that is mid-way between the Old Law and future glory, a stage of partial fulfillment. The images and symbols of the Hebrew Scriptures have been fulfilled but only partially. We look forward to complete fulfillment when the Lord returns. The Church, as the Second Vatican Council brought out so well, is a People still on a journey. What is characteristic of a people on a journey is that its situation is imperfect. It has to deal with inadequacies, failures, and dangers from the country through which it passes.

This is the picture of the Church that we find in so many of Jesus' parables, like the parable of the sower, the parable of the weeds and the wheat, and the parable of the good and bad fish brought up in the net. The Church in its present stage is a mixture of the good and the bad. It is largely composed of the half-converted. The Church does not just happen to be imperfect at times. The Church on earth is, of its very nature, imperfect. It is not yet the Church of God's final kingdom.

The lesson we need to draw from this is that we should not be surprised when we discover that the Church, this Body of Christ, this beloved Bride of Christ, will at times let us down, just as we will sometimes let it down. Its members are imperfect. Its bishops, priests and deacons are imperfect, its religious communities are imperfect, and so many of the things it does are done imperfectly. How should we respond to this reality? There is such a thing as legitimate discussion and informed questioning of existing practices as well as holding people in leadership positions accountable. Yet we should not get into the habit of useless complaining, carping, and criticizing. Nor should we allow the sins and other human imperfections of the Church to become an excuse for neglecting our own practice of the faith. We need to cultivate a deep love for the Church, and to be unfailingly thankful for this great gift that is the presence and activity of the risen Lord among us. In this way, we will continue to grow in our Christian life, and we will truly help our brothers and sisters who are the Church to continue the journey we make together, toward the eternal life that God promises us if we are faithful.